Praise and Kud

Jack Drakeford has written a very personal book about his more than 40 years of experience as a New Jersey public servant, starting as an Englewood city fire fighter leading through to his terms as Englewood's City Manager, Council President and School Board President. Mr. Drakeford provides his perspective on his career, where he overcame numerous obstacles to put himself in a position to help many, many people and help shape an entire community. Jack Drakeford pulls no punches in his highly frank memoir written, not only for historians, but as well for the new generation of individuals who seek to contribute positively to their community.

— Steven R. Rothman
Member of Congress
Ninth District
New Jersey

Jack Drakeford is a man of principles and uncompromised convictions. It was my delight to serve with him and learn from him as a councilmemeber in the City of Englewood, New Jersey. It was clear to me then and even clearer today that his love for public service is deeply rooted in his lover for this city, his family and his heritage. He has unapologetically worked on behalf of the least and left out.

Deliver Me from Those Liberals is just a sneak peak in the journey of this political giant. On behalf of countless numbers of lves that you have impacted we say "thank you" for your service.

— Dr. Vernon C. Walton
Pastor, Mt. Calvary Baptist Church, Englewood, New Jersey
Former Councilmember, City of Englewood, New Jersey
First African American Freeholder, Bergen County

Praise and Kudos for Jack Drakeford
Continued

A fast, sharp, analytical mind dedicated to the best interest of the community and people of all ages and walks of life—that is Jack Drakeford. He has been a powerful influence in the progress of important accomplishments for his city, county and state.

During the course of my career I served as administrative assistant in both federal and city governments. While working under Englewood city manager, Jack Drakeford, I came to admire his qualities of frankness, honest, sound judgment and outstanding leadership. He easily earned the respect of both his department head professionals and office staffs.

Behind his seemingly easy going manner is a complex person whose ambition has been the promotion of Englewood's education and economic development.

— Ladare Elliott
Retired Assistant to the City Manager, Englewood, New Jersey

As President of the Board of Education of the Bergen County Technical School District, Jack Drakeford was a Leader who understood his role. During his time on the Board, Jack provided vision and guidance, yet he never micromanaged the District's operations. It was this style of Leadership that allowed the District the creative space to develop opportunities for students that were years beyond what other Districts dreamt about. Thank you Jack Drakeford!

— Robert J. Aloia
President Board of Education
The Bergen County Technical School

"DELIVER ME

FROM

THOSE LIBERALS"

Politics through the Eyes of a Humanitarian

 JACK DRAKEFORD

With Damion Sanders

WELSTAR PUBLICATIONS
New York

Written by Jack Drakeford and Damion Sanders

Published by Welstar Publications, Inc.
Horace Batson, Publisher
628 Lexington Avenue, Brooklyn, NY 11221.
Phone: (646) 409-0340
Fax: (718) 338-1454
E-mail: publisher@welstarpublications.com
or drbatson@optonline.net
ISBN: 978-0-938503-12-5
10 9 8 7 6 5 4 3 2 1

Managing Editor, Kate E. Stephenson
Copy Editing, Book Design/Typography, Kate E. Stephenson
Text set in Times New Roman
Cover Design, John White

This book is dedicated to

Gazela Drakeford, my grandmother

and

Margaret Drakeford, my mother

It is because of their unconditional love that I had the determination to pursue my dreams.

I always knew that they were in my corner...

I thank God for the ladies.

FOREWORD

When I came to Englewood, New Jersey over 50 years ago, I heard a lot about Jack Drakeford. At that time he was a fireman in the Englewood Fire Department. He later resigned to become a Councilman for Englewood's predominantly African American Fourth Ward where I lived.

Over the years I heard about his involvement with the City of Englewood, but I did not get first-hand experience with him until I came to work for the city in 1982. At the time Jack was the City Clerk. I was hired as the Personnel Director. Within a couple of years Jack became City Manager. That's when the real war began!

When the residents got wind of his appointment all HELL broke loose. Some said he wasn't educated enough, some said he wasn't smart enough, some said he was from the wrong side of town, and some said in no way could a Black man do the job. Some Council members felt the same way.

It was evident that racism was raising up its ugly head and I was determined to bring my grandchildren to witness history in the making. The meetings were packed and all of the naysayers came out to oppose this appointment. But the grace of God was upon Jack's life and no weapons formed against him were able to prosper.

Needless to say, he proved them all wrong. Jack is a master strategist! I watched him negotiate and create more opportunities for African Americans and other minorities than any other City Manager in the history of the City. His negotiations skills and administrative skills were superior to anyone else and he did it all with integrity and a smile.

Struggles and negative criticism was not foreign to Jack but his ability to smile, hold his head up high while still encouraging everyone to their best, was who he was.

Jack brought a new meaning to the word politician. He truly, sincerely cared about the people and he had their best interest at heart. If an employee had family problems, especially if it was related to his or her mother, Jack would melt to butter. This did not make him a wimp. It showed his true heart and concern for his fellow man.

I learned many things from Jack. But the three most important things I learned from him were: 1. Regardless of what is going on in your life and around you, do not let anyone stop you from reaching your goals. 2. No one can be or do better to you than you yourself. 3. You don't have to set out to make any enemies, you will make enough just by doing the right thing.

I regard Jack with very high esteem. He sincerely understands and puts into practice that "YOU ARE YOUR BROTHER'S KEEPER!" I will always cherish our friendship and I truly regard Jack as a mentor. JACK, BECAUSE OF WHO YOU ARE, I INCITE YOU TO BE MY FRIEND FOR LIFE!

— Rev. Agnes McClendon

ACKNOWLEDGMENTS

One of my most loyal friends is Richard Sheffield. He showed unconditional support in all of my endeavors. I could count on Sheffield for political advice and to analyze the landscape of players. Sheffield may differ with me, but he didn't allow anyone to question my integrity or my determination to help my people. I will always be in his debt for what he meant to me and what I received from him for being my friend. There is so much history between Sheffield and myself, I could never forget him showing me the way and molding me into the man that I am. I will always be grateful for having him in my life.

INTRODUCTION

Why This Book, Why This Title

As early as adolescence, I knew I was strong willed; so did my grandmother. It's no shock at all that back talk was to be the prime reason I got into hot water. If I felt anything was unfair or I simply disagreed with her on a matter, it would be all I could do to keep silent. My natural impulse to rebut earned me so many lickings that any observer would be led to believe I felt speaking my mind was worth the whipping.

Unlike with grandma, my intolerance of the unjust has served me well in the realm of politics. It has been an invaluable asset in my fight against racial inequality. However, just like with grandma, my difference of opinion has gotten me into hot water my entire life.

I grew up in Englewood, New Jersey in a time when racial injustice and segregation were common practice and it would be twenty-three years before the Jim Crow laws would be abolished. As a young man I served on the Englewood Fire Department for thirteen years. Because of the shade of my skin I was overlooked for the lieutenant position for which I was well qualified. That type of blatant injustice clenched it for me. I quit with a retirement pension less than two years away. But I decided from that moment on that policy must change. And if I was going to change policy, I had to get to where policy is being made.

I am sure that at first glance at the title, you may assume that I am a conservative, Republican, Independent or anything but a Liberal. Quite the contrary. The irony is that I am, have been and will always be a proud liberal Democrat.

My political stance on equal rights for minorities has never wavered. So it comes as no surprise that I have fought tooth and nail my entire political career to make sure blacks receive equal treatment. What I find a bit more remarkable than the fight itself for Democratic progress is who I was fought by. That's right! My own party treated me worse than Republicans. Why?

I have found that so-called liberals are no better than conservatives because it all comes down to the agenda of Control for both. Like many conservatives, Democrats can, have and will use politicians to get in power. Yet, they will not put the politician himself in power.

I have written this book for the many people black and white who, regardless of socioeconomic status, have been victims of this "liberalism". My desire is that the reader knows that though I myself am a liberal, but according to the liberals of Englewood New Jersey, I was not one of theirs.

This book was not only written to give the perspective of a black male who was successful at obtaining political power but also to give the citizen a glimpse of the system from within. Of course, black people were not the only ones affected by the agendas of white liberals. In fact, whites have contributed largely to some of our major successes.

However, our nation's political history is packed with examples of both black and white, average and below average breadwinners who have suffered at the hands of our political leaders. These influential individuals have more often than not, offered an abundance of lip service and have displayed little or no humanistic values. I have observed that the so-called liberals of the north east have largely contributed to nothing but the detriment of minorities.

We can see the result of their "handy work" from Pennsylvania to Maine. Minorities are lavished with empty promises but given no real status in almost all communities, especially major cities where one would expect results. It has been my sole objective to demonstrate to everyone nationwide, that if given the opportunity, minorities could bring the necessary leadership to progress any process, especially governmental.

I strongly believe that a fresh outlook can change the trends in America, and allow minorities to reach their full potential if given a chance to compete on an even playing field.

I have chosen this title for much greater purposes than its irony. It is both a cry that accurately voices my distress with a needless battle I've fought my entire political career and a call for all peoples to examine and take action against the corrupt Democratic officials who represent or rather often misrepresent them.

I am well aware of the resignation of the American people caused by the corruption of its politicians.

We cannot turn on our televisions or listen to the radio without hearing news of some crime or misconduct perpetrated by a political official or how a major corporation received a slap on the wrist for initiating global catastrophe.

From nude officials on Craigslist to corporate criminal bailouts, our political system is in ruins. The enforcement of governmental checks and balances is an absolute joke. I know.

Ironically, the outcome of its future greatly depends on the actions of those who this system has spurned most. This battle belongs to those who have rightly turned their heads in cynicism and disgust, my black and brown brothers and sisters.

While the response of despair is justified, it is not profitable, and complacency is expensive. In fact, one of the most valuable lessons I have learned in my pursuit for equality is that scarcity and injustice thrive on the apathy of the people.

I am not only a living witness, but a prime example that persistence, hard work and compassion can overturn injustice. And although it is a piecemeal process, equality can be accomplished. My message is simple. Change is possible and it begins with you.

PART I: MY LIFE—THE FIRST 74 YEARS

CHAPTER 1: A GRANDMOTHER'S LOVE

I was born in May 14, 1937. My mother left me in the care of my devoted grandmother, Gazela Drakeford. Our household consisted of five members, my grandmother, me and three cousins. The love and honor she showed not only for me and my cousins but for herself as well has greatly influenced my respect for women.

She was a woman of diminutive stature, who took no tea for the fever and no funny business. In this current era of loose living, I can fondly recall that my grandmother believed in decorum. Throughout my entire youth I never saw another man sleep in our house. In fact, I was the only man coming through the doors to see my grandmother. What a sacrifice to make to hold true to her beliefs.

Although I came from a somewhat rough neighborhood in Englewood, I could only tell from my outside surroundings. My grandmother spared no expense in making sure I was comfortable and had all the advantages I could as a child.

Gazela Drakeford was an incredibly loving and giving grandmother. However, she was not one to be toyed with. Nurturing and generosity aside, if you crossed the line (which I did far more times than I can count) she became a strong disciplinarian.

Like any child, I acted out and got into bits of mischief here and there. In these moments grandma was never slow on the draw. I was caught smoking on one occasion and by the time she was finished with my backside, I felt like smoke had come out of me from both ends.

I had a serious penchant for speaking my mind, even as a child. That is, if I disagreed with something you said, I couldn't resist the urge to immediately set you straight no matter who you were. I've never been partial to the idea of people walking around misinformed.

If anyone tried imposing their ideas of who I should be on me, I would quickly let them know just who I was. I decided early in life that nobody, but nobody defines who I am but me. As much of a manifesto as this may have been, to grandma it was being flippant plain and simple. Backtalk, as they called it, was an offense that earned me my fair share of lickings. And in those days it didn't matter what parents instrument parents disciplined you with.

Grandma would be right there with a belt strap, extension cord, church-shoe—whatever she could grab in the immediate area. But I would never accuse her of being abusive. She simply believed that to spare the rod was to spoil the child.

But I grew up never wanting for anything. In fact, the extra attention showed to me by my grandmother resulted in a bit tension with my cousins. They were upset because while she was always a fair woman, the fact that she favored me was a bit candid at some times more than others.

Deliver Me from Those Liberals

It was as simple for me to get a car as a teenager as it had been getting a bicycle as an adolescent. During my senior year of high school my car began cutting off on me. So, my grandmother went down to the showroom and bought a brand new car for me as my graduation gift. I have often wondered how she could afford to make all those purchases. But I never wondered why. I knew it was to secure my confidence. I knew I was doing just as well as any of the privileged children in my community even though we were far from rich.

I knew without a question that my grandmother loved me. In her words and in her deeds she made it clear, frequently. She would say things like, "I love you," "I expect for you to be somebody," and "I know you're capable of greatness." I remember when I was about age 14, she sat me down for a talk and her exact words were: "If you don't make it, nobody else in this family will." Those words made such an impression me on that they still resonate in me to this very day. Knowing that she believed in me so strongly moved me to new heights of inspiration and aspiration. I was grounded in the truth of her statement. My grandmother's belief in me helped not only instilled confidence but birthed focus in me.

And yet, her revelation of faith in me was two-fold. It was as practical as it was poetic. Neither my mother nor grandmother graduated from intermediate school. My grandmother went as far as the third grade and my mother dropped out in the sixth. Yet their departure from the road of academics had been circumstantial and not one of choice or lack of aptitude. Grandma strongly believed in the school system. She was an avid believer in the sovereignty of the school board. If the board of education said it, that made it so. No questions asked. So school was a necessary evil.

But I was blessed, because in that institute of learning, I found others who saw the potential in me. I'll always remember what I was told by my seventh grade Latin teacher. She said, "Jack, don't let anyone give you any classes or courses that aren't related to academics. You're a bright young man and you have no business wasting your abilities in any other classes."

This assessment was a highly inspiring kick off to my high school years. With the combination of this teacher and my grandmother's encouragement, I excelled throughout my primary and secondary school and in the fifties I enrolled in college. I began taking night courses at New York University (NYU).

For as long as she was able my grandmother paid my tuition at one-hundred dollars per credit. To this day, I don't know how she did it. I was spoiled in many ways. I know that my grandmother wanted me to have every advantage possible, but I wonder if she wasn't also trying to compensate for my lack of parents, especially a father figure. I can never thank my grandmother enough for her sacrifices. But at the time, young as I was, sacrifice was not my concern.

Deliver Me from Those Liberals

As gifted as I was and as much support as I had, I wasn't completely above my circumstances. Like many boys who grew up without a father figure in the home, I got caught up. My irresponsibility put me on the fast track to fatherhood; I had my first child, a daughter, in 1957. And while being a young parent was far more taboo in those days than it is in American culture now, my grandmother, and number one supporter, never let me get discouraged or hang my head down. She spurred me to strive even more, not only for my sake, but my daughter's as well.

In my sophomore year, I was offered an employment opportunity in the campus computer lab assisting students. Only it meant working nights. I was hard-pressed to decline. Being a young black man with a family to provide for, the days of college had ended for me. It was time for me to join the workforce.

For a time, I worked three jobs just to stay afloat. While I was working nights at NYU, I briefly worked in a movie theater and also began a career as driver for a black owned cab company. As I recall, I was the youngest licensed taxi driver in Englewood. One of the owners, John Wright, happened to be the first black councilman in Englewood and the only Black Democratic official in Bergen County.

During those years I had the opportunity to discuss politics with John. I listened for hours with attentive ears as he shared with me not only his many victories but his horror stories about the political process.

Jack Drakeford

John gave me insightful perspective on the pros and cons of civil and public service. He felt that I had greater potential than I could achieve as a taxi driver. He would nag at me to join the police or fire department. But I had a special aversion to becoming a police officer. My primary issue with the police force was equality. I couldn't be a part of any organization that refused to treat everyone the same. If I was going to lock up a black man, I'd better be able to arrest a white man for the same offense. I knew I could never be a cop.

Still, John kept nagging me to start a career, one that could set me and my family toward a path of financial stability. My answer was steadfastly "NO." But John kept talking and out of habit I kept listening. The more he talked the more he made sense. I figured no reason being stubborn for stubborn sake. But I still couldn't stomach the thought of the police department. Instead I took the fireman's entrance exam. And not to his surprise, achieved the highest score among all other applying examinees.

At this time Republicans were in power. So, my friend and former employer used his leverage as councilman to get me into the department doors. His only concern was whther or not I'd be able to handle the job. That was the least of my worries. I was fully confident in my ability to take on any task assigned.

After much expected red tape, I finally received a congratulatory letter officially extending me the offer to join New Jersey's bravest. I was appointed to the fire department on July 16, 1959. This date marked the beginning of a life rooted in public service and the end of one spent in speculation and commentary only.

CHAPTER 2: SIR! YES SIR

The year was 1960, and having served five days shy of two years in the Army Reserves, I was drafted from Fire department into active military duty. To this day, I view that transition as one of the greatest in my life.

Yes, I saw and learned a lot about the world. But I learned even more about myself and others. I enlisted in the military with one purpose in mind, to serve my country for two years and return home. I knew it wouldn't be easy.

I began my basic training in Fort Dix. I was there during the worst recorded winter in forty-two years. We experienced everything from weekly blizzards to twelve-foot snow drifts. Most weekends we were assigned to base under strict confinement. Any soldier caught violating was brought before the Company Commander.

I made it my businesses to make it known just what an asset I was. I made sure that I knew every job in the operation. In event someone was sick or for other reasons unable to complete their task, I could step in and fill their shoes in a moment's notice. My superiors knew they could rest assured that I would be there capable of doing whatever job needed to be done, no matter what the level.

The free time that I did have in the military was spent alone. I had always been more of an introvert. I really wasn't into the things a lot of the other soldiers enjoyed. I didn't hang in the bars or anything of that nature. I was basically a loner.

Deliver Me from Those Liberals

Due to my prior experience, after the completion my basic training, I was assigned to the fire department at Camp Roberts, California. It was there where I was exposed to some of the most overt forms of prejudice and racism I have ever witnessed.

A civilian captain once addressed me as, "Hey, you!" Then he gave me orders to go out, clean up and carry all provisions needed to take the boy scouts camping. This request was not a particularly surprising one. The link between the military and the boy scouts has always been strong. On occasion, U.S. soldiers would mentor and occasionally take the scouts on outings.

The problem was I grew up a very proud child. If I gave you respect I demanded respect back from you no matter who you were. I was no different as an adult. "Hey, you!" did not seem a respectful way to address anyone, even a dog. I responded by telling him just what I thought. Things became heated between us quickly and I became a bit belligerent which resulted in a write up.

But I have never been an unreasonable or lazy person. I believed in doing my job and doing it well. This work ethic had gained me the favor of a sergeant who never had an issue with me or anyone else for that matter. I told him of the incident that happened with this particular captain. The two men had a relationship of which I had not been aware. I found out that this same captain was in charge of administering leave passes for the men in our company and had on more than one occasion given the sergeant beyond the weekly allotment of passes.

Sergeant stuck his neck out for me big time when he approached the captain and told him plain and simple, "If you take Drakeford to court marshal, I will have to testify on his behalf. At the risk of incriminating my own self, I'll have to inform them that you've been giving me these passes."

The captain threw out the court marshal but I found myself shipped overseas for 14 months.

During my tour of duty I was first briefly stationed in Germany. Then, my company was sent to Scotland on orders to deploy missiles from a nearby ground base. Things took a horrible turn immediately.

There was a malfunction with the trajectory of the first missile we sent up. And instead of it propelling forward, it came hurling right back toward us. I was in a truck in a nearby ditch overseeing the operation. We vacated as quickly as we could. Yet, fifty people including myself were stricken with panoline (a toxin which attacks and destroys the body's red corpuscles). Thankfully, none of us incurred any long-term health complications. But the incident reminded me how dangerous life can be.

Upon return to Germany, something happened that I've never forgotten. I had to share quarters with this white boy who may or may not have understood his comments could have been offensive. He welcomed me by introducing himself, then managed to fix his lips to say "We all heard that you were coming and with you being the first black that's ever been in this company and all, we're just wondering how you're gonna turn out." Of course, this asinine comment at first made me a little hot under the collar. But I had just arrived so I let go. What I wanted to say was, "If I were white you wouldn't have wondered how I was going to turn out!" But I understood to an extent that although tactlessly, he was just trying to tell me they had heard about me, that they had been told that I was coming, and that it was kind of a historical day for us all.

There was a black man in the German forces!

The irony is that with World War II having ended just fifteen short years prior, German-American relations were poor. Whether black or white, if you were an American soldier, the Germans didn't want you there. Yet, if you were black they liked you even less. I was one of the many thousands of black soldiers in Germany that signed petitions requesting that President Kennedy assign us to any country other than Germany. We wanted to be assigned to a country that welcomed and appreciated our presence. The fact is there were many who still supported Hitler. Many who loved him. To the majority of his followers he was the leader of the peasants. I came across German soldiers who had worked for him personally, and I'll never forget meeting one in particular who told me his exact feelings about his dead leader: "Look, Hitler didn't do anything to us, he may have done some things to other people, but he made us feel good because we had finally become somebody under Hitler's regime."

That was a defining moment for me. I've always been able to find the good in situations. (I don't think there was anything in my life that I couldn't find something positive about. My grandmother has everything to do with this world view. Her optimism for my life was contagious.) Regardless of whether or not I agreed, the soldier's point of view was at the very least, educational. Of this I am certain, that encounter has stayed with me and colored my political outlook. An insight into the human condition that governs self preservation and self interest generally above all else. That one conversation narrates the danger of inequality and the lengths to which people will stoop to reclaim a sense of personhood, even at the expense, and sometimes especially at the expense of someone else.

My experience overseas was life changing and throughout my days of service, while I may have debated a few superiors I never once had an issue with my fellow G.I.'s. This confirmed what I had known all along. I was born to challenge authority.

Before I knew it, fourteen months had passed. My tour of duty satisfied, I returned home.

CHAPTER 3: WHERE'S THE FIRE?

I returned to the fire department with far greater insight on people and myself than I had before my tour.

At the time I was the third black fireman in the fire department. And the only one that you could tell was black from a distance.

Though Jim Crow laws had been abolished, segregation was still commonly practiced. Black butts were not allowed in white beds. This made it impossible for any black men in the department to be on the same shift—we all had to share the one bed designated "black". And no one else touched it.

Because of this, it made it impossible for the black firemen to serve on the same squad. Years later, as mature firemen retired, one of the black males with seniority asserted his right to a choice bed, finally breaking the invisible color barrier. I mean to say, because whites still refused to touch a bed slept in by a black man, we were able to get more of our own people in the department. Based on the unofficial regulations we were able to fill the beds of retirees with more blacks.

I have never been able to tolerate being treated unfairly, nor have I ever been able stand by silently and be party to any assembly whose intent is inequality. I extend to others the exact justness I expect to be shown to me.

In fact, during my more seasoned years as a firefighter, there was a departmental discussion and the subject was whether or not we would march in protest against the then, fire commissioner.

Under his administration so many felt his hiring and promotion practices unfair and worthy of a demonstration.

My point of view on the matter was slightly different. I did agree that the matter of so many unworthy people being promoted under his jurisdiction was one of inequality. Yet, the only difference between this fire commissioner and all the others that had been practicing the same sort of favoritism over the years was that he was black. So, on the grounds that they were attempting to punish one type of inequality with another, I simply refused to participate. We hadn't marched against any of the past commissioners who up until that point had all been white, why should we march against this black commissioner?

My fire chief wasn't at all thrilled about my take on the subject, but he and everyone at the station knew by then that I didn't back down and was nobody's pushover.

The situation left a bad taste in my mouth and in other instances the chief angered me further. He had this tendency to yell for people that just irritated me to no end. I found it disrespectful for starters. He'd scream, "Drakeford, come here!" "Do this!" or "Do that". Until one day I reached the end of my tolerance for him and I said, "Look, I don't holler and I don't scream when I need you and I do not expect for you to do that when you need me. So next time you pull that garbage, be prepared. Because I will holler and scream back and I won't care who is around when I do!"

Well of course you know he wasn't pleased in the least to hear that. But I had been in the department for years by that point. My devotion to my job was evident to my superiors as well as my colleagues. Like me or not, my job was safe. And beyond our conversation that day, we worked together without further incident. But it didn't mean he had forgotten the experience, nor did he forgive it.

After thirteen and a half years of impeccable performance, and dedication to the department, I decided that I was overdue for promotion. I had expressed my interest in becoming Lieutenant to my superiors countless times. At length, I decided it was time to question the fire chief as to what exactly was the problem. To this day, his response still strikes me as one of the dumbest statements I've ever heard.

He said "Drakeford, I'm sorry but you're not officer material. I've been watching you and I'll be honest: you're too close to the men." Here I am, someone who's impartial, hard working and dedicated to these men who barely see their families while risking life and limb on a daily basis. And you have the unadulterated gall to tell me that I'm too close to the men? I was befuddled. And to this day it still doesn't make an ounce of sense to me.

What I learned about the so-called grading "system" the fire chief was using to determine which men were promoted would forever change the course of my life. One

Jack Drakeford

day a councilman from the ward that I currently represent went down to the firehouse to do a preliminary check and speak with the chief. He was still intent on getting me promoted to lieutenant. It seems that by the time he arrived the fire chief had already graded test papers from a previously given exam. Well, the councilman couldn't help noticing the blaring BNW handwritten in the upper right hand corners of select test papers.

He demanded that the chief tell him what those letters stood for but was given nothing but vague and evasive babble about certain tests having to be coded. The councilman's curiosity was far from satisfied. He could not get past the very likely possibility that BNW stood for "Black & White" from under his skin. One would have to question at the very least, why test covers would have handwritten codes if in fact the grading system was straight up? Why should any identifying codes be marked on the test papers after they've been submitted?

Disgust and betrayal don't begin to express the feelings that swept over me as the councilman recounted what he had seen that evening in the firehouse. In no time at all it dawned on me that my being overlooked for promotion after nearly fourteen years of devotion was purely one of race. And I said to myself, "No, You can't stay here! You now know all you need to about this operation."

When I turned in my resignation, my friends and colleagues all thought I was mad. They said, "What do you mean, leaving? You've got a family and you don't plan on staying?" My reply was very candid. "Actually, my family just separated from me, and yeah, I know it's a gamble, but I'm leaving and moving on because I refuse to live under these conditions."

The decision to leave a career into which I had invested nearly fourteen years time was a simple but not easy one. With thirteen and a half years of time served in the department, I would have to submit to a system I no longer respected for another year and a half in order to receive my pension. But for me it may as well have been another fifteen years. I was checked out. I could no longer devote another second to an organization that placed greater value on lighter skin than commitment to impeccability.

I had to move on.

My focus was now on the bigger picture like, how I could change things. I had a new goal in life, making sure that no one would ever have to deal with the discrimination and injustice I had experienced.

CHAPTER 4: COUNCILMAN IT IS

It was then that I decided that the only place to go was to city council. If I was going to change policy, what better place to start then where it begins? My mind was focused on change and fast. In the city of Englewood the neighborhood is broken into four wards. The residents of each ward can vote for politicians running for offices in their ward and in their ward only. Obtaining the fourth ward seat on the Englewood council was my new objective. I figured at least there I could address some of the changes that needed to be made within the fire department.

Ironically, after I left the department I was finally offered the promotion to lieutenant I had spent almost a decade fighting to obtain. But my stance was of course, that I had wanted it, earned it and well deserved it. The fact that they couldn't recognize it until my departure was their business. It now meant nothing to me.

Before I left I decided to bring it to the attention of the number two councilman, who at the time also happened to be the fire commissioner. Somehow he geared the conversation towards explaining which departments were the most important in his opinion. Because he was always dealing with planning, naturally he valued the planning board most. But he left my concerns far from addressed. He was wrapped up in the planning aspect. And my chief concern has always been employees getting a fair shake. The conversation reminded me that other people's goals aren't always your goals, and I would have to do the work myself.

With time served in the military, nearly fourteen years in the fire department and the advice of the friends I had made along the way, I had the right credentials for the job. My advancement on the road to councilman was mainly dependent on my making the public aware that I was running. It also just so happened that my predecessor, Councilman Vincent K. Tibbs, who had been quite ill only had one more year left to his term. I so wanted to be knowledgeable about that aspect of government, I the good fortune to have met with him at least five times before he expired. Well, I ascribe to the adage "strike while the iron is hot." I told myself, that I couldn't let another year pass. I would do it right then or not at all. Who knows if this chance would come around again? I made my interest and intent for office distinctly clear to the people.

I had the complete support of the black community. To gauge this, I insisted upon having a mini convention. I have always believed that the power lies with the people not the politicians. It doesn't matter what intention I state, without the people's support I'm dead before I get off the ground. A lot of politicians may not care, but the fact of the matter is the public knows when they lack popular support.

Throughout my life I have always been able to count on the support of women. Campaigning was no different. During the special election for fourth ward councilman, I had the good fortune of meeting a sweet, gray-haired, elderly black woman by the name of Rosetta Crawford. Ironically, this little old woman was one of the two most influential women in Englewood. Who could have known that I would gain the favor of one of same two women that spearheaded Councilman John Wright's successful campaign? I am not sure what it was about me that inspired her but she loved me to death and supported my every move.

It so happened that the fourth ward councilman's challenge was held on a Sunday. Unfortunately for me, I was scheduled for work. And although representation is key to winning for all candidates, my duties simply would not allow me to attend. Well, little Mrs. Crawford came to me at my job and extended an offer that to this very day is worthy of my gratitude. She said, "Jack, look. I know you're not able to make tonight's councilman's challenge. But what I'll do is go and represent you." I was so touched and inspired by her offer to represent me that it felt as if all the breath left my lungs. I graciously accepted her offer which I realize now was more a declaration of her faith.

Still desperately wanting the opportunity to represent myself, and full of anxiety about the forthcoming poll results, I waited for what seemed like an eternity. Within two hours time, I received a phone call from Mrs. Crawford. Her exact words were, "Jack, congratulations, you won two to one!" I was overjoyed and after some consideration I began to view my not being able to attend the challenge as a blessing in disguise. It was only after winning the election for councilman without having been physically there, that I knew beyond a shadow of a doubt that I had the people behind me. Oddly enough, in one year's time I was now the boss of the very same fire chief who told me I wasn't officer material.

The year was 1973, I had assumed my office. I had countless people who believed it was in my best interest to accept the appointment to council without going through the mini convention. Preferring the option of being the people's choice, I refused to go that direction. And for that decision, I believe I was the first black councilman from my ward who refused to be appointed to my first round before being elected by my people. My view was if I could not get their support there was no way I could ever get the job done. I am a firm believer that every now and then you've got to raise some hell if you want to get things done. But if you're raising hell and you don't have the drive or the staying power, then you're better off cutting your losses and call it quits.

I believe a prime reason I had the support of my people, outside of the fact that I was one of their own, is that when I applied myself to a cause, I would be out there fighting for it no less than one-hundred percent of the time. That's the only way I know of effectively getting things done. Besides keeping your hand on the plow, it is also critical to stay vigilant and to not only expect the unexpected but (to some extent) be prepared for it. Because

A, anything that can go wrong will go wrong. And B, those who do not like you will block you at any opportunity.

Before beginning my term I had to be appointed by the City Council to complete formalities in order to make my transition from to fireman to councilman official. An ordinance has been passed in Englewood preventing all employees from becoming elected officials while remaining on their previous jobs.

In the end, I went from a middle income salary to a stipend of about $300 a year. Obviously, a yearly salary that meager would not cut it. They figured lowering my wages would be a natural deterrent from my interest in the job. They figured wrong. I quickly found my success in real estate and through it, was able to support myself until I made the transition to city person.

The first issue I had to deal with when I was appointed was that I shouldn't be council liaison to the major departments because I was inexperienced and should take the necessary time to understand the operations of being a city official.

From day one, I was unafraid to oppose my fellow Democrats and candidly question their motives. They quickly discovered that I wouldn't be anyone's pawn and decided to withhold from me any more of their already-flagging support. When the liberals saw that their approval was neither necessary to my survival in office nor essential to my political progress, their annoyance turned to hatred.

Deliver Me from Those Liberals

The liberals resented me for every inch of momentum my political career took independent of their support. I would fight the rest of my political lifetime. Which was fine by me. I knew and believed 100% in what I was fighting for, my people. And my Grandmother always said there's nothing wrong with a good fight.

When I first went into politics, I'm certain the politicians in my district assumed I was delusional. I'd tell them "I'm here and I am the balance of power."

The leverage that I've obtained my career I got by ignoring political labels and partnering with whoever had the best interests in mind for my people. I didn't care if he was a Republican, Democrat or whether he yellow, purple, or blue, If they're for my people we could work together. After all, my whole purpose of being in office was not only to protect my people, but also to make sure that they would be better off than they were before I got there.

When I began my first term as fourth ward councilman, I immediately tackled what I viewed as top priority, hiring people and making sure my people were given a fair shot. I worked closely with the budget committee to make sure that when they started talking about federal funding that they didn't forget to talk capital funding also. They would constantly argue with me, telling me I wanted too much.

One time we were debating the cost of restoring a particular neighborhood in my ward. I told them point blank, "If you didn't allow this area to be run down the way you have, then we wouldn't qualify for urban renewal." Nobody wants to "qualify" for urban renewal. In essence, it's like admitting you were careless and are now in need of a bail out.

My philosophy was if you didn't care about a neighborhood then anything is liable to happen to it. And the "happening" to it is nothing good. So, I was the community watchdog. And the fact is, because of it not only did the community respect me, but I was able to hold positions of power based on the vocal strength of that community. Having the support of the public to the point it actually pushes you ahead is extremely rare. It virtually never happens, even with white officials. Seeing a white man at the top of the helm in the town in which he was born and raised is a rarity. Gaining the support of the people is one of my greatest achievements.

All too often, politicians make the mistake of assuming they have begun winning public support due to the crowd's response to the grandiose claims made by them in their campaigns. While promises are a great foundational starter for rallying supporters, they are just that, promises.

In my experience, people ultimately put their trust in your dedication and results. I firmly believe the public stood behind me was because I was able to show them just where I could make a difference in terms of their quality of life. Under my administration we built one of the best low and moderate income housing projects in the city of Englewood.

Because it was all brick, it was very low maintenance. However, quite a few members of the housing authority thought that we had to be insane to spend $40,000 per unit at a total of 100 units. My rationale was simple. I knew it would be more economically feasible, overtime. Because honestly, how often do you need to replace a brick?

The people saw my commitment in everything I touched. And believe me, it was my intent to touch everything I could in the time I was given. My hands were in everything from bettering housing and increasing job opportunities to improving the school system. In fact, at the time New Jersey public schools were listed as top in America, I was president of the Englewood county school board.

In my experience a leader must earn the confidence of his people. While the price of the public's support comes at a cost specific to each leader, regardless of what that cost may be, it is never paid by any other means than a three step "lay-away" plan: The promises are the initial payment, dedication the second, with results being the last and most powerful installment.

In all my years of civil service from the military to council, I have stood flatfooted on the principle that, people come first. The job of a civil servant is exclusively linked to the needs of the public. I'm certain this simple fact is hard for even the dullest person to miss, especially since the name also implies the job requirements. So naturally, it puts us through a range of emotions, from hopelessness to anger, when we see civil servants who even make it as far as the Oval Office only to perform the exact opposite of what is both civil and service.

Though there are a number of political parties, and wide variety of political views, there are two, and only two types of politicians. There are those that are dedicated to improving the quality of life for others at the cost of themselves and those hell-bent on improving their quality of life at the expense of others. Too often we see the latter type among our nation's leaders. If we truly want the people to know that we're fighting for them, they've got to see it. It is the duty of the politician to make it known to his people that they're not on their own, but there's somebody out there and that somebody's ready enough to take on anybody in the system.

Everyone in New Jersey who knew me knew that I stood for my brothers and sisters and of that there was no question. When it was time to discuss the matter of funding projects I would constantly fight for most of the money to benefit urban renewal. While others felt that most the capital money should have gone to the other three wards. I took the position that it was due to city negligence that my ward was in such bad enough shape to qualify for urban renewal in the first place.

Within two years, I became Senior Democratic Council Member. I must say that the Council President that

I replaced was one of the finest people I've had the fortune of meeting. He was a fair man. But more than that he had such genuinely humanistic qualities that he stood apart from the majority of politicians I had met. Under his leadership we in the fourth ward council made remarkable strides.

He made quite a lasting impression on me. I made it my business that when I took over the momentum remained unbroken. In like fashion, I made sure that everyone was treated fairly and given the benefit of an even playing field. Still, not everyone was pleased.

I encountered a political group from the third ward known as the "Kitchen Cabinet," a powerful group of elderly women who had the power to decide which men obtained positions. Some of these women were teachers, some simply citizens with power. And some, for reasons I did not yet understand, did not like me.

They felt they should have determined who the Council president should be. They felt that since I hadn't fought for the position in 1975 when it was available, I had no right to fight for the seat in 1976.

What this particular group didn't understand was we (meaning the City of Englewood) had a black mayor, which they had railroaded out in order to place one of their figure-heads in office. They had no idea that I had already been audited beforehand by an official who questioned me on my political posture as well as where my support would come from.

I had already been unanimously elected by the council. The price they made the third ward council person pay was criminal. The "Kitchen Cabinet" resorted to not only harassing but threatening him. And when the time came for his reelection the group used every underhanded method they could imagine to get rid of him.

This set off a tradition that continued every time a white, Democratic council member supported me, no matter what the issue.

I served as Council President for one year and then was told that the City Clerks position would become vacant. Of course, the fight was on. Not only members of that particular third ward group but a few scattered members in other wards including the Forth ward began fighting to deny me the opportunity to serve a city clerk.

CHAPTER 5: SIGN, SEAL, DELIVER!

I had just run for and been elected for a three year term for forth ward councilman. I was now considering the City Clerk's position. This meant I would have to run city-wide for two terms of three years each. At this time, no black official had run city-wide and won without a Republican split in their party. I believed I could not only run but win my first city-wide election. The city clerk at the time felt strongly that no one would be a better candidate for the position than me. Now, he had been serving as city clerk for over twenty years. In his words, he identified with me because we were both from the other side of the tracks.

He said, "Jack, you should run for the office. Not only do the people love you but you have the character for it and you've been through the ringer." I was moved by his affirmation. Over the years of working side by side with him, he knew all too well the many instances where I had been over looked or treated unjustly. So, he assured me right there on the spot that I would have his full support.

The other contributing factor of course, was that my party wanted me out. I was defiant of everything that they stood for. And oddly enough, after all that time around them, to this day I'm still not sure what they stood for. What they said was not necessarily what they meant, and that annoyed me the most. They took the same oath of civil service as I did. Yet, we practiced two completely different sets of principles. I have given many examples of the roadblocks I encountered, and can recount more. To this day it's remarkable to me that the folks who were committed to getting rid of me most were the members of my own party. Little did they realize, they were doing me a favor.

Not only did I run and win my first city-wide election, but at the time, I received the highest vote count in local elections than any other politician in Englewood.

But this would be yet another victory for me that would not be had without strife.

The mayor and the fanatics from the third ward wanted the city clerk to run three times to achieve five consecutive years in order to become a tenured clerk in the city of Englewood. This made me the only municipal clerk in the State of New Jersey who would have to be appointed or elected three times to achieve tenure. The council pointed out that it was within the statute even though I had to threaten the Council President with litigation.

As a result, I took a drastic cut in salary in comparison to the preceding clerk. This was inconsistent with normal practice, but at every turn the liberal wing of the Democratic Party stopped at nothing to express their dislike for me. To me this was nothing more than another attempt to penalize me for my lack of conformity and my vehement refusal to esteem them with the fawning to which they were so accustomed.

I was elected city clerk and received power over the city seal in the fall of 1977. I remember thinking that

Deliver Me from Those Liberals

Englewood wasn't at all ready for its first black city clerk. I believe I was the first candidate—black, white or otherwise—to obtain the city clerk office in a citywide election. Again it was important to me to curry the support of the people, not just hobnob with the political elite. The people of the Fourth Ward and Englewood proper have always known that my interest is their interest because I have always returned to the people for support.

My duties as a city clerk were very similar to those of a historian, recording and archiving municipal documents. I acted as both the secretary of the governing body and secretary to the city corporation. Not a legislation went through without my knowledge and my signature to authenticate it. The city clerk wields the city seal, validating all important actions and filing them into the record.

It was the perfect position for someone interested in being in the thick of it. In fact, the city clerk's office is the hub in the wheel of government. Without the official keeper of records, government would descend into chaos. Even those that hated me couldn't get around me. And that's what made the city clerk such a powerful position.

The fact that I was only the third clerk in almost 75 years in the city of Englewood speaks volumes about the distinguished nature of the office. Holding this office of ancient and abiding importance has been was one of the most notable accomplishments in all my years as a public servant.

Yet, not everyone was thrilled about this milestone. My second wife at the time could not conceive of why I would possibly consider such a position. Her view on the matter was that I was doing such a fine job as councilman that by moving to city clerk I was turning my back on not only my people but all forth ward residents to whom I had given my all. I tried my best to explain to her that desertion couldn't be further from my motives.

It was much to the contrary. I explained my new role was like being the historian. As the only keeper of the records, and the most overall experience, I was the one in command—in power. It was just matter of me finessing a way to use my leverage to the advantage of the people. She couldn't get it out of her head that I had somehow sold them out. I know she was not the only person who failed to see the bigger picture. But I was unperturbed and still as driven as ever to serve my people.

On one occasion I arrived very late to an important meeting of the budget. A previous neighborhood meeting I was attending had wrapped up later than expected. I knew that my presence there let the people know that I was involved and they were far more important to me than anything else. I arrived at the budget meeting unbelievably late. They were just about fifteen, maybe ten minutes from wrapping things up. But I was there long enough to know that the subject of discussion was terminating employees.

And as late as I was I objected and said, "That's not necessary to get things done," By now I had seen the system at work. I knew that any and all efforts to "trim the fat" would definitely target minorities first.

What few people know is that minorities, as a whole, have a lot more seniority in different places than whites. However, unless the minorities are civil servants, they don't have the leverage to determine the rules. To make a long story short by the time I was finished I was able to discourage them to them from eliminating the DPW (Department of Public Works) because at that time that's where most of the minorities were. There was absolutely no way that would ever take place on my watch. I had to go in and reshuffle the operations. In the process, I was going to do my best make certain the minority workers weren't exclusively targeted.

Yes, while some people did need to be let go, I proposed that it not be done through firing but organically, through attrition. Besides, it was not my thing to fire people, it never has been. Today's administrators are far less discriminate in terms of downsizing and will fire an employee with seniority or otherwise.

In American culture we are presented with rules, we embrace those rules after closely scrutinizing them for fairness. And we are generally let down after the appraisal.

The word fair is so arbitrarily used, so diluted by underlying incentives, that its true intent has become mythical. While I believe in what fair implies, I am wary of those who speak on the subject. I believe the purity of word has been soiled with entitlement.

What they were proposing for the DPW was anything but fair.

The Department of Public Works is the environmental division of New Jersey responsible for sanitation, garbage recycling and park upkeep and management. I knew that the budget committee's agenda was to fire all of the minorities in that entire department.

They had no meaningful connection to my people. Nor did they have any desire to. So naturally, whether they had jobs or not was inconsequential. Using budget inflation was the perfect cover for them to cowardly justify terminating hardworking people. I had to help by putting things in perspective for them. I pointed out the fact that we were probably one of the few cities in the entire county that had an engineering department.

So, we eliminated our engineering department instead. The reason being that aside from getting a salary for running the DPW, they were still getting their cut of 10% - 20%, for not only all the engineering projects that the planning board approached, but all the engineering projects that came out of the city.

They were all making out quite handsomely until we arranged a contract that would pay them a decent salary, but not give them what they had been used to getting. The notion of terminating poor people in order to advance the well-off to a financially better position is a complete disservice of not only your office but the public.

Deliver Me from Those Liberals

Some employees get huge raises and others don't. Then they attempt to justify why one got and the other didn't. To this day, the same problem persists in Englewood. Just this year the big wigs all got a 10% - 20% pay increase, while the other employees received nothing. And won't be receiving anything next year either. There's something's very wrong with that. My experience as a city clerk showed me that as city manager I could have the kind of power and support needed to oppose prejudice and corruption within payroll administrations.

CHAPTER 6: A DOUBLE DOSE OF DRAKEFORD

In 1984 after seven years of service as city clerk, there was a council meeting and my name came up as a candidate for city manager. Well, a councilwoman who was not thrilled at the news to say the least, who was standing directly behind the podium at the time says the word "Nigger". After the smallest glitch of silence the meeting resumed. It was almost like someone had hit pause for a second. Of course, no one addressed her. It was almost as if it never even happened.

I laugh at it now. While I find nothing remotely funny about ignorance, looking back I realize that such a blatant, tactless attempt to offend me was more than likely employed in hopes of triggering an emotional reaction in me that would result in my own sabotage. This was the eighties and although American society wasn't as so-called "racially progressive" as it is today, being openly slurred in a professional political sphere was still unacceptable.

Strangely enough, I didn't feel the need to respond to such a low grade attack. I never have. Yes, this was the first time I had been candidly called a nigger in a "professional" arena but along my path I had encountered many openly racist and bigoted individuals. However, my personnel director was very upset that I had been treated so. Being a woman in that same era, she could identify with all the discrimination and the prescriptions of inferiority.

Though honestly, racist comments neither affected nor shocked me in the least. I honestly wasn't expecting anything less. I would have been very naive to believe that I wouldn't have to face my share of indignant white people in my attempts to fix a system broken in their favor; a system already treating blacks like second class citizens.

I knew the powers that be didn't want a black man to become city manager. It had never even entered into their minds. If any Democratic councilman in their district was going to further his career he needed their seal of approval. Or so they believed.

Now after eight years the city was without a city manager and the Council advertised and hired a headhunter for the position after six months. Certain members of the council began asking me to consider taking on the position. As City Clerk I was also acting City Manager whenever the official City Manager was out sick, on vacation or if the position was vacant. Since the city had seen three managers in less than eight years, I had plenty of time to understand the City Manager's position and the relationship necessary for the city to function. And I knew I was qualified for the job.

I decided to throw my hat into the process for City Manager. I reasoned it would offer me the best opportunity to help my people move forward and that it would be far more advantageous to pair with position my preexisting office of city clerk.

I must state that prior to the vacancy in the City Manager's position I was a municipal chairman in Englewood, head of the Democratic election process for election candidates. When I ran for Municipal Chairman I was threatened by the liberal wing of the Democratic Party.

The reader should be aware that occupying both seats was not unlawful but at this time very rare. Years ago a politician could serve in two or three different capacities at a time. While simultaneously occupying both offices of city clerk and city manager is still permissible, it is a bit more difficult today. Holding both offices was beneficial in that it would enhance my reach and effectiveness as a public servant.

However, there were certain Democrats who viewed the leverage provided by both offices as a too much power for a black man. If elected I would be one of the first African-American politicians to simultaneously hold both the positions of city clerk and city manager and the possibility of that set off the Democrats like the scent of blood to starving wolves. I was now seen as a potential threat to their bottomless appetite for power and that's when their attacks intensified.

I was told that if I ran for this position I would be blacklisted and would never again be able to gain any advancement in the city. They did their best to keep that promise. This time they went after the white Democratic supporters who would vote for me to become City Manager. They even went to the extreme of threatening to campaign for a Republican to get them elected over any white Democrat that voted for me in the City Manager election.

Deliver Me from Those Liberals

Despite their threats I obtained the support and Democratic appointment necessary and in 1984 held both the seats of city clerk and city manager. But it would come at the expense of two laws suits served by, you guessed it... liberals. Regardless, I needed both because it's nearly impossible to do anything without leverage.

It's all about leverage. I honestly would never have taken the city manager's job if I were expected to relinquish city the clerk's position as well. I had to keep the city clerk's position because I had tenure among other things, and no one could hassle with me. I had everything I needed in terms of talking to or dealing with the governing body, independent of them of the governing body.

Everything I did was in order to make things happen. You couldn't just do something simply because you wanted to, no matter how noble your cause. Many pieces must be put into place to accomplish real progress.

I remember it taking up to four and five years to arrange all the variables in order to make certain projects happen. My patience was long, I didn't mind waiting. But I knew no amount of patience could ever replace the pace at which progress is achieved by through leverage.

I was already the city clerk and I could play the game of politics well.

Many people ignorant of public government and many within elected office, underestimate the role of city clerk. The power to wield the city seal is a great tool. In the seat of clerk, you see and validate every change in the town governance. Nothing gets by without your symbol of approval. I was in the position to affect many legislators and officials. I was able to do anything within the limits of the laws, and that was a great deal.

Of course there were liberals at my side questioning not only my merit but also the legitimacy of my holding both offices.

I was taken to court not once, but twice by members of The League of Women Voters. While the LWV is nonpartisan as a political organization, there were certain liberals within their administration who sought to have me removed from the city manager office. They fought to appeal my position as city manager. At this time the appellate (appeal) court was Democrat controlled.

However, there were also those who knowing the repercussions stood up for what was right. On the panel there was a Democratic Caucasian woman who not only found me faultless but respected and believed in my character. Her fellow Democrats threatened to ruin her political career she called their bluff. Only they weren't bluffing. I told her, "Look while your support is unmistakable and greatly appreciated, don't vote for me. I don't want to be responsible for them killing your bright future in politics." I knew that they would make good on their promises. And they absolutely did. When the time came for reelection in her ward the Democrats voted in a Republican rather than put her back in office.

Deliver Me from Those Liberals

The general public has no idea just how spiteful and calculating Democratic officials can be when crossed.

They were upset with me not because I had done anything illegal. Although the legal actions they took against me imply otherwise. It was allowed because one seat was an elected position and the other was appointed. They were upset that holding both offices took an amount resolve and public support that they didn't have and felt that I as a black man should been further from having. So, they were extra peeved with me because it was permitted at the time.

So, I cannot say outright they took me to court simply because I was black. While I felt a great deal of prejudicial sentiment while serving as a councilman, I had also received backing in various ways. So while my race was a factor that created some roadblocks, I cannot definitively say that it was behind the ire of some Democrats at this juncture.

I would do disservice to my party to say that the root of this litigation was because of my being black alone. They'll at least tolerate anyone who's complicit. My conflict was because I was not only black but uncontrollable, the story of my life.

When it comes down to it, it was really me and my mouth again that had me in the hot seat. But they were far more PC about it. They said their reason was political.

Or rather, it was that I was too "political." I couldn't argue that point. I found it to be an ironic one. Yes. The prosecuting attorney had drawn up the charter for the city which showed that I had relinquished the Democratic Municipal Committee for the city of Englewood.

I cannot say that I am apolitical. Only, I feel like it most certainly goes without saying. I mean, there I was, sitting in the top Democratic seat in the city, was I not?

However, the judge said, If you didn't want it to be political matter, then you wouldn't have the charter," Because it was a special charter, which allows for a political appointment. The judge told me if I didn't want it to be political matter, I could have had the normal charter, which doesn't allow for politics. But instead I chose to pick a political concept (my letting go of the Englewood Democratic Municipal Committee).

I lost the first case I fought at the appellate division. I lost the second as well

In the end, in both cases before the general practice court of law and the appellate division court, the verdicts were in my favor. It was legally declared that it was well within my rights to maintain dual offices.

After being taken to court by members of the Democratic Party twice in the attempt to have me removed from the city manager's seat, I was finally able to assume my duties uninterrupted. In one year's time, my potency as city manager was evident to all. Yet, it came as no surprise to me that my doubters weren't lining up to extend their support. I never expected to win them over. But they did realize that I could do the job, and do it well. That didn't mean that they would admit it, but I knew they knew.

When I obtained the position of City Manager, Englewood had the highest tax rate in Bergen County for over forty years. By the time I reached my two year mark in office we reduced our position to third, then fifth and eventually thirteenth in the county. Our financial rating went up from A to A+ which improved our borrowing ability at a lower interest rate.

I had real goals as city manager and I would say mine were quite different from the others. For instance, at one point the city's black employment rate plummeted from 60% to an astoundingly low 20%. Raising the minority employment level has always been a top priority of mine.

However, my concern was not merely with them obtaining jobs but having positions also. I made it my mission to convince people that minorities were just as adept at performing these job. And I am proud to say that out of all the other things of which I was accused, never once was I accused of hiring someone incompetent. Any minority I employed was proficient in any task they were assigned. I stood staunch on my principle, that any minority that applied for a position had a fair shot. If not fair, then at the very least a decent shot. Because without the right amount of support "fair" can be a bit tricky. Now, that is not to say that one would earn any points with me based on skin tone alone. Heaven forbid! That's the exact direction I was steering away from. Rest assured that they had a keen eye out for that type of nepotism (as it pertained to people of color). But without a doubt, if you came through my door and were you were a minority, I was watching like a hawk to make sure that you were at the very least, treated equal.

The importance of being flexible as city manager is a matter of relativity. It's all according to what you as city manager call flexible. Because the term flexible just like the term fair can have numerous implications. When I say a city manager should be flexible I mean and I believe that they have to be open minded and compassionate.

There's way too much riding on your ability to be reasonable. When you bring a cause before the state and federal government then you've got to have some leverage, and you have to have some sensitivity, because without sensitivity, what's the point of having leverage as a civil servant? Without compassion, what's even driving the desire for such an advantage?

That's why I always say that you have to have a temperament that allows you to see things as they are, not as you would like for them to be. That is the importance of flexibility. Much like the bamboo shoot in nature demonstrates, if you're willing to yield then you can move in many directions without being broken by the winds of change. If you're ultra-conservative you will be stuck in your posture; if you're a liberal, you usually you just talk about how much you're going to do.

In all sincerity, let's look at both at New York and New Jersey, for starters. To this very day it's extremely difficult for minorities, especially blacks, to break into the system at certain levels. I'd say that speaks volumes about how subjective flexibility is in today's political arena. You can be the greatest thing to walk into their office since the doors opened for business, if people do not have the flexibility to put aside their own agenda and do what's best for all parties involved, it matters not what you have to offer.

There are also instances wherein the one who has been violated must exercise a certain type of flexibility also. Say the minority is now in the seat of control. Now here comes this person from 10 or 15 years ago who may have openly perpetrated an act of racism towards them. My question is not only how long do you hold it against someone for having been racist but as an authority how long do you hold that person back from gaining upward mobility? The answer is there is no barometer.

I remember a black sergeant I once had in the police department who was brought up on charges for brutality. Not he himself, but he was present during the abuse and lied for his partner to the point of making a statement in the newspaper in his support. I told him he would never receive a promotion from me.

Jack Drakeford

I didn't care how good his record was. I was appalled that he could even begin to form his lips in denial that his very own sisters and brothers were being brutalized. For about 10 or 15 years he nagged me about recommending him o the mayor for lieutenant. I told tell him point blank "Look, I'm not making you anything so forget about it!" Eventually, I began to question my resolve on the subject. I had a talk with myself and said, "Jack, how long do you really hold out on somebody?"

At the time, I had also white police lieutenant whose name was on the list for racially related misconduct. And I had to decide as to how I would deal with the two. The chief of police would make recommendations to me, then after reviewing the factors, I would mentally prepare myself before addressing the officers. If I was not in the space to prepare myself, I would have to hold off on making any decisions. Racism is far too delicate an issue to address haphazardly.

I had a policeman of the force whose father called me up and asked, "Why would you promote somebody to a position higher, knowing that they were considered a racist?" I in turn I asked him I said, "How long does it take for someone to prove to the public that they've paid their debt and see life from a different perspective?"

I said, "Ultimately if the chief is willing to stick his neck out and make this decision, I would have to trust his judgment. Because in the end, I'm holding him responsible for the operation."

Deliver Me from Those Liberals

You can't appoint people to positions that affect the public and not listen to concerns that the public has about your decision, even if you totally disagree with the concept or whatever the concern may be. In the end, I finally retreated and so both of them ended up being pulled off of the list of problems that relate to racism. I believed in being objective and working to resolve issues as evenhandedly as possible.

However, not everyone in my party embraced my diplomatic approach. I encountered this one man who was black and a fellow liberal. And he gave me a solid chunk of his mind. He told me I was playing footsie with the whites and conservatives and accused me of much more than I can or even care to remember, because I couldn't listen to that type of nonsense.

When people have accused me of being unfair, I've always taken it with a grain of salt. Not because I am perfect. But I have always known what I stand for and that beyond a shadow of a doubt I have tried to be as fair as I can be when dealing with everyone. I didn't treat anybody any differently than I wanted to be treated myself. So from that perspective I think I was a pretty fair manager. I didn't cast you in a certain light because you were from wherever or because somebody knew you. I evaluated people based on whether or not they had earned the right to sit in their seats, and that's not an easy task sometimes because there are people who will test your last nerve.

And many people have tested my sense of fairness while pushing the boundaries of my patience. Many a person has come into my office with a complaint about a colleague. My response has always been the same, "hold on one minute," as I called the other person into the conversation. There truly are at least two sides to every story. When those two sides are separated and you can never discover the truth. I have no problem with someone airing a grievance with me. But I also want to hear what the other party has to say. When you hear all sides of the story you can better understand what really transpired.

I was only rigid when it came to making sure that people did the right thing. Not what they wanted to do, not what they felt they should do. I remember I had one lieutenant who would not stop hounding me about giving him a promotion. When he had taxed my last nerve I asked him, "Why should I give you a promotion? You don't even know who your boss is. You cater to the mayor. I'd advise you to go to the mayor to get a promotion, because you won't get one from me."

They used to think I was irrational but that's the way I felt. Don't try to tell me that you are ready to advance if you can't master the fundamentals of respect and honor for those who are your superiors.

I ran into the same officer on the street one day. And immediately, he jumped back to the same subject of promotion. "You just refuse to make me captain, don't you?" I said, "And you just refuse to listen to and know who your boss is. Don't you? So why would I even entertain your thoughts at all, if you can't respect your superior? We're paying you to follow orders not to give orders."

That's why people used to say that if Drakeford called you into his office, brush off your resume because you're gone. But I would only dismiss you if you stepped out of bounds and didn't have a legitimate argument. A man would have to be either cruel or foolish to come to such a severe conclusion without thoroughly examining all the variables. So to a degree, I was easy.

In fact, I was so easy that for a time, they were able to get away with paying me less than the city clerk and city manager before me because they came from a seemingly plausible position that I was getting paid what the offices were worth. I was told that I would have to occupy the position long enough to build worth and establish a wage level. So of course, with no established wage level in that particular area, I was vulnerable.

I had already encountered this as a councilman during my transition to city clerk the liberals attempted to strip me of my longevity and the time and experience I gained before I made it to the city clerk's office. So I knew that they were attempting to shortchange me and they couldn't do it legally.

I wanted to avoid headaches so I allowed it... for a time. I also knew that it was a tactic employed to discourage me from office. But the moment it got down to zero hour and there was only one other council member left from that deal, I wrote my supervisor a letter stating that he would not only have to raise my salary and provide me with monetary compensation for having reduced it, but that I would also retain my longevity. Or else was I taking him to court, point blank. I knew he couldn't get away with that. I was an exemplary employee with tenure. I played it smart getting in the door, but in the end there was just no way I was going to allow them to my treat someone of value and dedication like trash. As a result, no litigation was made. They gave me the money I was due. And that's when I became one of the highest paid blacks in the county. I was making six figures during the late '80's and '90's.

Although there were times that have I felt highly motivated by certain injustices to file a law suit against the city. I am most thankful that a diplomatic solution had been reached before things became ugly. I have always preferred using other, cleaner, methods when dealing with those who cause conflict.

Not only have I found better ways of handling these affairs but in suing the city, especially as a public official can gain you a fair share of enemies. And if you think I'm referring to the defendants, think again. There's always Citizen X, laying in wait to say "Look, I knew it! I told you politicians don't care about us. He's just like all the rest. He came and got something for himself. But what has he done for us?"

Deliver Me from Those Liberals

I recall when my human resource person asked me "Jack, I noticed you drive a small car. Why do that when you're such a respected figure?" My reply was "Because I'd like to stay a respected figure. I don't believe the majority of the public could handle seeing me in a big car. If you want to see them raise hell, then let me pull to work in a Mercedes Benz. I bet you there would be no end to the accusations."

And to a large extent I could understand the skepticism. After all, it wasn't as if the minority of corrupt politicians made any it easier for the ones that were out there fighting for the people.

When you're dealing with people, you have to deal with the humanistic values. There should never be a moment that you as a leader make a move that will affect the people and you don't question how. The core concerns that are on my mind when making a decision in the interest of the public are, why I'm doing it, how it will affect the people, whether it benefit them in the future, does it give them a fair shake now. There are so many variables that you must to take into consideration before making a decision all the while, trying to be as fair as possible in the process.

CHAPTER 7: THE BOARD OF EDUCATION?

While still serving as City Manager I was appointed to the Englewood Board of Education. Again I was targeted by the liberal Democratic wing that brought me before the council on suspicion of potential unethical behavior.

I was taken completely off-guard by these unfounded claims. I was able to challenge the right of the ethics committee to handle the case on the simple grounds that I had not yet even accepted the seat. I was now being accused of unethical practices however, the commissioner found no cause. This initial failure to have me removed from the board only fueled the fire. They continued to harass me, putting forth all diligence to ensure that my reach remained as limited as possible. They fought hard to against my advancing to a position of power.

When I first came aboard I recall two white males that were debating over who should be president. I made it clear to them and all other Caucasian members that if they wanted my vote I would have to be vice president, but that was that last thing they wanted.

So, I voted for one black woman for presidency but not for her running mate because she was a member of a white female organization that supported the white liberals who assembled to stop me from becoming City Manager and took me to court attempting to have the vote overturned. This particular organization had the support of this woman because she was complicit in that she never challenged their position for supporting the legal action.

Deliver Me from Those Liberals

As for the two white males, (let's call them Board Member A and Board Member B) both developed a deep hatred for me for the sake of my eliminating either from being considered for presidency. Board Member A resigned. As for Board Member B, I reached the end of my patience with him and ended up telling him off in a closed session. This resulted in him openly becoming my adversary. His one intention was now to bring me down.

So, he researched all my actions as city manager and tried to discredit me in the eyes of the public. Ironically, Board Member B, who was also the former council president when the mayor and council were in the process of determining terms the office of elected officials due to a charter change, had defended a white businessman who in one year's time had grossed nearly a million dollars. Board Member B even went to the extent of releasing a statement in the newspaper, defending him and attesting to his honesty. He went on to say that he also had no problems with the amount of money he was earning.

I, on the other hand, grossed approximately $75,000.00 through my business as a consultant for the city and also as part of my terminal leave package. Yet, he tried everything within his power to discredit me.

Well, the next school year I was elected president of the school board and the Kitchen Cabinet group began showing up at board meetings. This group hadn't been involved in the ten years prior to my becoming board president. They began to challenge and disrupt board meetings by questioning and directing as much slander as possible at the board and board president.

This continued for the entire school year but I was reelected board president for the second year in a row. They continued to complain about everything they could think of but the board pressed ahead.

In my second term as board president, I aligned with the new superintendent and task force made up of twenty municipalities in East Bergen. The purpose of this was to eliminate racial imbalance in the Englewood School district. The East Bergen task force presented a plan that I thought was ingenious. The plan: a new approach to addressing racial imbalance in schools where communities are integrated, yet the schools are not. I embraced this plan wholeheartedly.

In my three years served as board president we moved to redistrict elementary schools. It was my business to make sure every student would have books and that the district was moving toward the direction of having a uniform curriculum in place. And to top it all off, a model high school (Dwight Morrow High School) university high school for excellence. I hoped that it would end ten years of legal battles at the high cost of quality education in the Englewood school system. My desire was to help create a high school for excellence and hopefully an integrated school system based on equality and opportunity.

However, my best efforts still weren't enough to have me reappointed to the Board of Education, even though I was president. The mayor had a particular white male in mind for the position. Now, the school system consisted of 95% black and Latino students, yet he appointed board members who would support his position that the board president would be white. These board members also supported his decision to appoint another white member to the school board, making the representatives of the funding committee all white from the school side. The city side, the mayor is white and the city council was all white except for one black member on the financial committee who had been determining the funding for the school for at least two years.

So, four out of five members of the financial board were white yet the school system was approximately 95% minority. There was not one Latino representative on the school board of seven members. But this procedure no longer surprised me. It followed what I now referred to as the Mantra of the Liberals: Let us lead you.

I must confess that there was another reason for me not being reappointed to the board. The State Commission on Education created a Bergen County task force to come up with a concept to desegregate Englewood's Dwight Morrow High School. The mayor had manipulated the system so as to be selected as one of the representatives from Englewood, despite the fact that he would have been the only mayor representing the twenty municipalities on the committee.

Jack Drakeford

Yet, it must be understood that the only two blacks on the committee were from Englewood, the superintendent and me, the board president. I believe that the mayor and his staff members felt that the school board of Englewood needed white representation and a white perspective simply because its board president and superintendent were black.

In their opinion, we were not supposed to be able to work with the nineteen white communities to come up with a workable concept to desegregate Dwight Morrow high school that acceptable to all twenty communities rather than one. They most likely believe this because we as minorities have more often than not, accepted the liberal "Let us lead you" approach, taking what is given even if grudgingly.

The Bergen County task force came up with a school to meet all students' needs, a very progressive concept to desegregate Dwight Morrow high based on the "university high school concept with grades 9-12." The concept involved the following; we would be a satellite school for the # 1 math academy in the county. Every student would be eligible for the first two years of college tuition-free. It would bring the school system up to the state of the art in technology.

The curriculum concept was consistent with the 2000 Education goals. The board of education with the support of the mayor failed to endorse this concept because it was not viewed by them as a plan. It did not have all the

Deliver Me from Those Liberals

"details "a plan would entail. Yet, this concept was very detailed in terms of its goals and objectives.

In my belief, it was the folly of the task force for believing that Englewood's Board of Education could be capable (even with the assistance of the mayor and a handful of do-gooders) of perceiving the difference between a concept and a plan. They made the mistake of thinking that they had the ability to take so worthy a "concept" and begin creating a workable plan tailor-made for Englewood.

I believe that Englewood should have been put first. Because before I even became school board member, I had resolved that students were not just our top priority, but our only real responsibility. Once again, we have a demonstration of the liberal "Let us lead you" philosophy hard at work.

I have witnessed the behavior of Englewood Democratic Municipal chair people and have found them to be quite chameleon as it pertains to their character. They seem to think of themselves as "White" and "Black" when it's beneficial to their needs. From my experience, they have one objective: use and discard as many people as necessary to fulfill their agenda.

CHAPTER 8: RETIREMENT?

With a total solid thirty-five years spent in the civil service field, I decided that I needed to recharge. I retired from my posts of City Manager and City Clerk. It had been a momentous ride full of great progress and significant setbacks. And I was simply burned out.

Power doesn't mean anything if you can't use it to the best of your ability. Sleepless and brought to the brink of obsession with the committees, meetings and abundant responsibilities, in 1994 I hung up my politician's hat to enjoy a much deserved siesta.

Even though I was off the field, I never really stepped away from the game. I couldn't allow myself to be out of the loop. I may not have been in office, but I was still very much a part of the Englewood community. The politics of the town are just as much a part of my fabric as anything else. I made it my business to stay informed and involved.

During discussions with representatives and other people about town, I started to hear and see things— changes in the city that were not to its benefit. So much of the effort and work that I had put in to create a more even playing field was being dismantled little by little.

The people that supported me seemed to be calling me back to action.

Therefore I knew that they were going to support me if I returned.

The support of the public and the support of the people is how I reclaimed office. It wasn't any great master plan, it was name recognition, my past practices, and my track record that spoke for me in the end.

I had more experience than everybody else. 40 years experience to be exact. And the fact that I had illustrated that I not only knew the job, but could perform its functions in and out.

I assumed my inherent position on providing blacks and minorities with job opportunities an seeing to it everyone got as close to a fair shake as possible. Sadly, I knew the stand for equal rights would still be a relevant one.

I knew my people, were still getting the "short end" of the stick. The facts were in black and white. How could officials possibly claim that they were giving my people a fair shake, when out of the top twenty-six positions only four are occupied by blacks. In my opinion that means you don't exist! Where's the equality in blacks and minorities representing nearly 80% of the student population, and the school board not having a single black or minority among them? I find something to be seriously wrong with that. My campaign was largely focused on the double standards and racism that were openly practiced.

Jack Drakeford

While the issues I addressed in my campaign were certainly among the most pressing, I still had the matter of convincing the public I hadn't lost my ability.

I simply stated my record. I talked about what I stand for, and my intentions. After all experienced or not, you can't expect people to know your character by simply looking at you alone.

In my opinion, the average politician really doesn't take time to validate the views of the public. Many carry out their campaigns with an air of entitlement, believing all they have to do is declare what they want and they will automatically receive it. Things just don't work that way. I am leery of the politician with the "Don Juan" complex, believing he has some ability to woo people or convince the public that he is the right person for the job.

Not to my surprise, during my second time around running for city council, I did not have full party support! I remember a particular young lady from, Montclair's Teachers College who lived in Englewood. She was a very eloquent speaker who was well-off, so of course she had people working for her. She used her resources to the best of her ability to and tried to give me hard time. But she knew she couldn't hold be back.

Otherwise, nothing else was standing in my way.

I jumped back into action and with the support of my people, have been serving as elected councilman for the second time, since 1999.

CHAPTER 9: BOARDS, COMMITTEES & PROJECTS. OH, MY!

I was approached by Victor F. to bridge the gap making the L.V.W (League of Women Voters) my advisory committee. It is no secret that one of my top priorities has always been is making sure all young people are given a chance to be successful. Through my partnership with them I was able to follow through on my ambition to not only ensure that the youth got the tools, classes and opportunities needed to grow in their respective fields, but also help improve the quality of life of for the families of Englewood.

I served on the Hospital Board of Englewood for fifteen years. My sole purpose for coming aboard the H.B.E was to help eliminate discrimination in hospital services, employment and community services. I was there to also to see to it that minority doctors were given equal opportunity to serve on the hospital staff. I've fought for bettering systems such as the clinic program, the ambulatory care program and to reduce the cost of emergency room visits.

In 2009 I was the president of the Bergen County High School Board. The very same year we became the number one school for math and science in the nation and number three in the world.

One of the groups that I worked with was the executive committee of the Chamber of Commerce; I took them on and made them my executive committee for my finance and budgets.

Jack Drakeford

And the reason for that was I wanted to stay professional, I didn't want to lose sight on the professionalism, and I knew that all of them were professionals, they were either bankers, or heads of corporations, or whatever, you name it, so they knew their stuff. I couldn't have pulled any wool over their eyes, and I wasn't trying to, that's what ... one of the set of things ... that was why I had the chamber.

I am also a consultant for the Labor Union Local 108 RWDSU. I presently serve on several boards. I am on the board for Habitats for Humanity of Bergen County. In addition to my being on the Englewood Housing Authority, I am also Board President of Bergen County Technical School which has been honored by Intel. as the best math and science schools in the nation.

I believe that two of my greatest political achievements were becoming the Chief Executive Officer for the City of Englewood and City Manager. Primarily because I am a town native which is a rarity in most cities. And my single most personal achievement is my two daughters and two stepsons who are truly dear to me.

I enjoy helping others and making a difference in my community. As a leader, I believe that my management style differed from others because of a culmination of my life experiences. I believe that many of my finest moments are when I am discussing the challenges and possibilities of politics.

Deliver Me from Those Liberals

Some of the greatest moments of my life were my international experiences, which ranged from going to Russia and assisting with changeover to Free Market Economy and my visit to Israel in order to gain a better understanding of Israel's challenges and survival techniques.

The mayor recently appointed me to the budget committee. I am hopeful, that I may be able to take it to new levels of accomplishment.

But you can never be too certain. The success of any group is dependent upon the drive of the individuals within it. For better or worse is all relative to who's on the committee.

I've been in this profession a long time. Everyone in Englewood knows me by now. And name recognition is worth a lot. Most politicians tend become high-minded and begin to think themselves above the very public that they've sworn to serve. Which for the life of me, I can't comprehend.

How can you be a servant and think yourself above those who you're indebted to. If I were an up and coming anybody who wanted to be an official of some kind, I would make sure that I had the public support. Because they're the ones that are going to vote for you, vote on your position, vote on a lot of things that are going to have a direct effect on you.

Jack Drakeford

If you have troublemakers on board, then the progress of the group is sure to be hindered. This is exactly why I candidly told the mayor there was one person that he appointed on the board whom I would not side with. To which he replied, "Well, Jack, if I must make a choice between you and him... it's you, you will be appointed." Of course, I graciously accepted. And yet to be frank, a portion of me felt entitled to it. I had paid my dues. I was treated like I was a nobody for a long time.

Since my return from retirement, I've been a councilman for longer now than my first time around before I became city clerk. The strides we have made in Englewood and the Fourth Ward over the past decade make me proud, but I know there is still much more left to do.

PART II: MY HEREOS

CHAPTER 10: THE THREE GREAT LEADERS

As a young, black man born and raised in a white suburban area, I not only witnessed but lived under the oppressive influence of the local conservatives that were in power. Under their regime I saw divides being initiated that not only succeeded in separating blacks from whites but even worse, blacks from each other.

Sadly, even our religion failed to be exempt this division. Like any black person, I knew I was being cheated out of my basic human rights. But like most, I didn't have the first clue what I could do about it. I am not only acquainted with feelings of optimism one the feels the moment before taking on a worthy cause, but also the feelings inadequacy and resignation.

Due to my interest in black leadership I had the good fortune to read the about life and teachings of fearless individuals like Marcus Garvey at an early; age to be young in an era of great activists and humanitarians like Adam Clayton Powell, Martin Luther King and Malcolm X. I hold these three men as the three great leaders of all time. They are, in my opinion, the very best examples of how to live the life of a public servant.

They professed what I knew in my heart all along, that "black people should be free to determine and follow their own destiny." That was all I knew at the time. It was all I needed to know to start me on the path of making a difference. I have learned no opposition to justice and equality can withstand the power of passion and determination.

The primary reason I can confidently refer any leader of the people to these three men, is because of their integrity. Each of these men lived a lifestyle that unflaggingly opposed inequality and racism, and because of that their lives were in constant jeopardy. They never knew from day to day whether they were going to live or die.

Yet each knew one thing for certain, and that was the difference between justice and injustice. They knew that people were being treated unjustly and to them it was unacceptable. While each had his own faults, unique approaches to equality, civil rights, and spiritual beliefs, each agreed on two fundamental principles: one man can make a difference, and to do so requires no more than faith in something greater than yourself.

CHAPTER 11: CHARISMA

Adam Clayton Powell, Sr. was the pastor of Abyssinian Baptist Church in Harlem, and a politician who did more by himself than the whole black congressional caucus did collectively. In 1945, he became the first African-American from New York ever to be elected to congress. He represented Harlem, New York in the United States house of the representatives.

Powell was a charismatic young leader who rose to prominence during the Great Depression of the 1930's. His dogged commitment to issues like housing and employment for minorities earned him incredible popularity among the residents of Harlem. From his vibrant speaking style, to the unrelenting intensity of his voice, he was a magnetic leader who attracted others not only because he was in touch with, but moved to action by the struggle of the common man.

After obtaining the chairman seat on the Education and Labor Committee in 1961, he began to cry out for the rights of those who were yet without a voice. He tackled issues like equal pay for women, desegregation of schools, education and job training for the blind and hearing impaired, and a host of other civil causes.

One of his biggest achievements includes his instrumental role in making lynching a crime punishable by federal law. My desire to not only have the political reach, but also the drive to fully exhaust it helping others has been inspired by Powell's example. He was indeed, his brother's keeper. He was not against whites, but for fairness. He once said: "Unless man is committed to the belief that all mankind are his brothers, then he labors in vain and hypocritically in the vineyards of equality."

The man had a vision in terms of his people, and he was not going to give that up. In fact, he was so dedicated to obtaining equal rights for minorities that, he was willing to risk losing popularity within his own party. The Democratic Party's reluctance to fight for civil rights caused him to look for solutions outside of his party.

So, he moved to endorse president Dwight D. Eisenhower due to his progressive outlook civil rights, for his second term in 1956.

Like all men he had his faults, but he was a seamlessly fearless leader who wasn't worried about losing his job, who wasn't worried about impressing people. He was outspoken for the people, with the trust of the people.

CHAPTER 12: VISION

Martin Luther King was born 1928 in Atlanta Georgia. He was a Baptist minister who followed not only in the spiritual footsteps of his father but of his grandfather as well.

Like most children, King was able to distinguish inequality at an early age. Unlike many, he grew up to become a beacon of hope and leadership that would catapult the civil rights movement. As a child, he grew up with a Caucasian best friend who he was permitted to play with side by side yet was forbidden to learn with. It struck him as odd that while he was taught at home the importance of treating others with equality and respect, it was a principal not practiced much place else.

In the coming years, King encountered instances of racial inequality from the bathroom, to the ballot box. During this uphill battle for revolution, he saw the face of every form of hatred from scores of unlawful arrests to physical violence against his person, being stabbed during one of his book signings.

Yet, despite beholding the injustice all around him, King was more moved by the promise of things his eyes had always wished to see.

After becoming an epic voice for the civil rights movement, he was viewed as a threat and treated accordingly. But even having his house firebombed and being the target of several violent attacks didn't deter him from his one objective: equality for all. He knew the job he had to do went beyond his own ability.

And it was his gift of making people see just how possible the impossible was that made him such an inspiring leader.

King has such an immense following, such a way of rallying support that the only conceivable way of stopping him was to either pay or knock him off.

If Adam, Martin or Malcolm were out for self interest, they could have made a fortune. Sadly, a sellout will always be in demand. I shudder to think how the civil rights movement might have stunted if Dr. King had allowed his voice to be bought.

CHAPTER 13: POWER

Malcolm X was a revolutionary Muslim leader who believed in unity between Christianity and Islam. He realized as long as you were black, you'd be harassed whether you were on your way to church or to mosque.

In Malcolm's 1964 "The Ballot or the Bullet" speech, he stated that we as a race were not anti-white but anti oppression. And if the white man didn't want us to be anti-him, then he should, "stop exploiting, oppressing and degrading us." The title "Ballot or the Bullet," was not chosen by Malcolm merely for its clever play of alliteration, it was also highly suggestive of the desperation and the militant "By any means necessary" approach he felt was essential for black equality.

His message was not one in favor of violence as many have misconstrued. Rather his position was one in favor of what was most effective. I believe he clarified this with his statement, "Nonviolence is fine as long as it works." He was a revolutionary who was very intellectual and methodical and, when he felt the time was right, he wouldn't hesitate to take action. In the same speech Malcolm said, "If we don't do something real soon, I think you'll have to agree that we're going to be forced either to use the ballot or the bullet. It's one or the other in 1964. It isn't that time is running out—time has run out!

It was not only Malcolm's no-nonsense stance for black equality that made him a threat. What frightened the oppressive white ruling forces even more was that his militancy is what won him the ears of the people and the support of hosts of other powerful black activists including Dr. Martin Luther King Jr.

In his January1965 speech, just one month before his assassination, Malcolm made a statement that added the kindling to my already-burning desire to see blacks obtain their God-given right to equity. He said "Nobody can give you freedom. Nobody can give you equality or justice or anything... you take it." That declaration has not only resonated within me but has greatly influenced my outlook on how minorities ought to approach obtaining equality.

CHAPTER 14: MALCOLM AND MARTIN

Malcolm X and Dr. Martin Luther King Jr. were raised in two completely different worlds. Malcolm X (formally Malcolm Little) came from a poor family. He was a self-taught man who grew up more street wise than institutionally educated. He did not become scholarly until he and an acquaintance were arrested and were both sentenced to a seven year sentence for burglary.

This slowed Malcolm down a bit and gave him some much needed time for introspection. It was in prison where he began to harness his greatness and build on his intellect. Malcolm X arguably rose to his greatness through the discipline and sheer determination he found in his spirituality.

Martin was raised in a stable home setting where education was priority number one. He came from a well-off and well known, middle-class family. Outside of segregation laws, Martin's parents were able to provide, safety and comfort for their son.

Yet, the two share striking similarities. Both were the son's of Christian ministers. Both grew to be among the most influential and memorable freedom fighters of all time. And tragically, both were taken from us at the young age of 39.

Though Dr. King and Malcolm X may have differed in backgrounds and their approach to equality, I think Malcolm and King were both militant. It was King who said "If you're 40, and have no cause for which you'd be willing to die, then you're dead already."

And of course we can hardly argue the militancy of Malcolm who made the statement that we as blacks would gain our equality... "By any means necessary."

CHAPTER 15: FIELD & HOUSE NIGGERS

The sullen truth that we as black people have been divided amongst ourselves is no shocking new discovery.

According to Malcolm this division was initiated during slavery when the slave masters planted an insidious seed in our minds to believe that there was a difference between us. The deception was that the closer our complexion was to theirs the greater the value placed on their lives.

In addition to having us believe a lighter skin tone was more acceptable, we were also conditioned to believe that the more submissive we were the more favoritism would be shown. With this type of division planted within the collective mind of the black race not only did the self-hatred that we still see today emerge, also the separation of a people whose greatest allies have always been each other. The result was the categorization of blacks according to their skin tone, physical build and temperament.

According to Malcolm, The house niggers were the maids, the cooks, the butlers and "mammies". The field niggers were the ones out there doing the work, picking the cotton, bailing the hay, all other sorts of physical labor. It is my belief that today's political arena presents a powerful argument validating Malcolm's slave distinction.

If those standards were to be applied now, today's politicians would fall into either of the two categories. I would personally consider myself of the field variety, not only having been in the "field", but because of my zero tolerance for disrespect and foolishness. When such instances arose, I handle them orderly. The irony is, that while the house nigger once took pride in and enjoyed his position of intimacy with the master, the very same advantages are still appreciated albeit, closeted.

Of course the benefits of such brown-nosing are enjoyed publicly, but they will publicly deny all intimate connections to the "boss man" when questioned. Today, the title of house nigger is held in the same regard as being a "sell out." Who today would say, "Well, yeah. I'm the house nigger!"? No one, of course. There's a very short line to the podium where people admit having sold out.

PART III: HOW I SEE IT...

CHAPTER 16: HOW I SEE CURRENT POLITICS

It should come as no surprise that the political leader's primary obligation must be to the people first. There's no way around it. The role of any good elected official is to be an honest servant, attending to the needs of public who without which, he could not possibly have obtained such authority. Ironically, I have witnessed this type of individual as a minority in the current political sphere.

The current state of politics is that of a circus. Sadly in not every member of this carnival is a willing participant. There are those who seeking to make a change have unwittingly joined the political big top. In their haste they have accepted a favor from fellow politician with a hidden agenda, and are now bound to wrong by an attempt at right. We also must contend with gender and racially based biases that are unabashedly practiced day to day, and the political orientations that advocate in perpetuating the myths and stereotypes that mold our still-forming perceptions of current politics. This is how I see it...

The Wall Street Dilemma

I believe the government could have handled the Wall Street crisis a number of different ways. For starters, they could have ensured that the working man kept his job which essentially keeps the money circulating in the system. This would have been a prudent approach simply based off the knowledge that in today's economy the average working-class person must spend far more than they can save in order to survive. True, they are in no position to splurge but are scarcely in any position to be monetarily conservative. I stand firmly behind the notion b that job security should have been priority number one.

Of course, we've got to bail out the big corporations, there's no question about that. This is necessary if only for the sake of them having the ability to hire the people and get them back to work. But if you've noticed that was far from the first thing that they acknowledged or took care of.

In fact, they have been taking care of every other kind other demand rather than making sure that the little employees keep their jobs. If anything, there was far more effort put in to making it seem as if the potential for job recovery was there for them. Instead the focus was on making sure that the corporations and businesses, both small and large, had the money necessary to stay afloat. And there has since been no attempt to make reparations to the people.

Since the bailout and the massive financial setback incurred by the average and below average breadwinner in wake of it, things have been business as usual. I totally disagree with that approach. In my opinion, what was done was the equivalent of saying businesses and corporations come before the people that build them up.

In my understanding, no programs have been implemented in order to provide real assistance or rehire the people impacted most by this dilemma. There was at time when it was understood that you had to have people working in order to circulate money. How can you spend what you don't have?

Women & Politics

Women are the toughest of all creatures, because they never waiver. If they've made a statement you can rest assured they won't give up their position. For this cause, I find it so ridiculous that throughout time men have used all diligence to withhold their feet from an arena where their ability, will do the most good.

Though, I suppose it is the insecure that fear competition most. The way I see it, on average, men have a tendency to see how far you're going before they will commit to your cause. Women on the other hand, usually know from the beginning whether they can or cannot commit. That's why I put a lot of faith in women.

Yet, I am not biased. I've seen what women can do. Women do not back down. Women are unafraid, and will not skip out while owing a debt to anyone. Their concern not unlike men is being in charge. You will scarcely find woman who is disinterested in being in charge of things or at the very least, her own life. I haven't run into too many women that didn't want to run their own lives, especially the women in politics.

Jack Drakeford

Politics and Media

To be frank, my time as a political figure has left a bad taste in my mouth for both parties. It is a sad truth that order to win elections you must be named as one or the other. But, our so-called two-party system is a joke.

People turn on their television sets and flip through their newspapers looking for political facts, when the irony is that it's the media that influences to a great extent what we the people actually believe is going on in politics. Most of what the press prints regarding politics is biased, the information is cherry-picked and doesn't really inform the American people as to what's really happening.

So, if you're backing a politician based on the Daily whatever, just remember the press is fickle. In politics your greatest week in office can be your first. Just ask President Obama.

President Obama

President Obama has walked into a sandstorm. Dealing with intense pressure and scrutiny, Obama deserves an enormous amount of respect, but I also have my reservations.

Take for instance the Race to the Top education initiative, in which schools are competing for the highest ranking and funding is allocated accordingly. However, the problem with this initiative is that while it's highly workable, it's being approached from an economic, financial point of view. There is not much leeway for experimental ideas regarding money (even potentially sound ones) in the crippled state of economy which he has inherited. And when you're talking to working class American people the assurance of tax dollars is everything.

Before President Barack Obama assumed office our economy was already so deep in the hole from borrowing money that he really has a hard time explaining it away. Yet, he has no choice to ask for tax dollars. The money has got to be taken from somewhere.

I think that under his plan, American children are very likely to benefit. But the Race hasn't been sold to the American people. In my opinion the president doesn't have a very good public relations group. It seems as though he handles his own public relations—but he's only one man and president is his primary role. That's why it's so tough to get the word out and obtain the people's much needed support.

CHAPTER 17: HOW I SEE THE JOB

I've always believed that the key to office politics is not to play them. I've always lived by my own set of morals and rules of conduct which include such basics as "treat others the way you wish to be treated". Over the years I've learned a number of things about getting the job done (and doing it well) the hard way, and I hope I can spare someone some of the trouble (or rather, give you a heads up on the consequences of stirring up trouble). I don't purport to know it all, but I've been around the block a time or two and seen some things. This is how I see it...

Power

In my capacity as city manager, I called all the shots. I not only determined whether a position was needed, I also appointed everybody with the exception heads of departments. Therefore, I had virtually unlimited power. My goal was to have power. Power changes everything. I would I tell people that I would have no problem living under a dictatorship...if I were the dictator. Who'd want to live like that otherwise?

But once I got power, it was exclusively about making a difference. The main thing about having power, is understanding how to utilize it. Power is not something that is given to you, you have to take power. I am not speaking about taking power in an imperialistic Stalinesque fashion. We've already addressed the issue with dictators.

I mean, if you are to have the type of power that makes things happen, you must pursue it with an eager-to-

85

earn mindset. What you can accomplish is only limited by your hunger. I knew no one was going to just roll over and say to me, "Here, Jack, I want you to have this power." It doesn't work that way. You've got to pay your dues.

My Work Ethic

Working your way up in terms of value at any company requires more than just hard work. Remember people of low paying positions work just as hard, and in most cases harder than the average person. Of course, I don't speak against the value of hard work. But hard work alone does not insure progress. And while it is a principle of success, it does not stand alone. Elevation also requires ingenuity. Aside from the commitment to a job well done, if one is truly seeking to increase their value, at least an intermediate knowledge of other jobs within your organization is a definite plus.

I made it my business to know the job of everyone with whom I was on staff. My focus was always on making sure that I was indispensable. In any professional you may seek to enter, government or otherwise there is no way to perform your job impeccably without knowing it in and out. And you must never be afraid to speak your mind especially as it pertains to let people when they're wrong.

I remember one day my assistant city manager, Mrs. Elliot came to me and she said, "Jack I've been trying to get the information your requested back to you in time, but all I've been getting are excuses, from the reception department" I told her not to worry and that I'd get things straightened out.

Well, the next staff meeting I had, consisting of department heads and division heads, I said to them point blank, "If Mrs. Elliot sends you a memo stating that she needs information just remember that she's speaking for me. She hasn't asked you for anything other than what I've told her *I* needed. So, if I can't get through to you verbally, if I have no problem sending the same message through your paycheck. I'm not here to play silly games. I have to get the job done. And the only way I can get the job done is by making sure everybody plays their role."

That's how I handled business. I was as fair as I knew how to be, but I didn't take any garbage from anybody. And I didn't back off anybody, especially if they were in the wrong. I didn't care who they were. I wasn't afraid of losing my job. I stayed with leverage, no matter what job I had, whether it was councilman, city clerk or city manager. I always wanted to know where my leverage was.

My Difference in Management Style

I had my hands occupied with committee meetings, budget planning, neighborhood restoration and many other projects simultaneously. Yet, my eyes were always open. I watched everything from the numbers of employees (that was always important to me), to the office layout. I knew who was doing their job and who wasn't.

Deliver Me from Those Liberals

You couldn't just you just tell me you were doing the job. Being an on hands type of person, I'd walk through an operation and I would just observe. I would never disturb or say anything to anyone.

For example, I could spot an employee lying out on the grass when they should be working. In those cases, I didn't even want to know who was. I was far more concerned with finding out who their boss was! Why leave the employee exclusively at fault. Heck, if I could get away with stretching out on the grass because my boss wasn't seeing to it I handled business, I'd do it too!

Everyone more or less, got one shot with me. If they decided to ruin it in some way, it would be very difficult to get another. I've always treated the occupation of civil service with the utmost respect, gravity and professionalism. And I have expected nothing less from all who come under my employ. I can always tell when an employee is being dishonest.

Never Let Em' See You Sweat

As badly as the antagonists from my party wanted to, they just could not get to me. I wouldn't allow it. And even when they came close to plucking my last nerve, I made sure they never knew it. The main thing I made sure of make sure was that I never reacted to the foolery.

I always kept calm and took collected approach to trying situations. To me being the balance of power meant that I set the pace. There is no way that you as a leader can have a calming effect on your environment if you don't impose the focus necessary create peace as opposed to being lead into chaos.

The Games People Play

I happened to be in the position to hire employees, when the drug epidemic first struck Englewood as well as all of America. I showed no leniency for that kind of foolishness. As far as I was concerned, if you failed at the drug test, you couldn't be hired, I just wasn't going for that. Unless you could furnish some evidence that you had been truly rehabilitated, you weren't going anywhere that required my say-so.

My main objective was not only to be fair but to make sure employees felt they were being treated fairly as well. Unfortunately, not all employees felt that I was always fair, but there were some things I just would not tolerate.

Games were chief among the list of my pet peeves. I remember a human resource officer came into my office and said, "Jack, you know Aaron said that he felt like he dodged a bullet when he came in earlier and that you weren't in. It just so happened that Aaron had manipulated the drug test system and had managed to successfully avoid taking it although he should have within the first three months and had now been there a total of six months. I was well aware the fact that he had failed to make the necessary steps to be tested by design. I told the same officer that he could tell Aaron to clean out his desk when he did emerge

Deliver Me from Those Liberals

I meant business and I believe that's why they used to hate me so. They would say that I arrogance sometimes. I would to refer to it as confidence. The truth is that in my position it was impossible to be a gentleman at all times. Especially due to the fact that the weight of getting things done fell squarely upon my shoulders.

If was there to do a job and if I felt like you weren't doing yours or attempting to get over, I had no issues with setting you straight. I got no joy out being anyone's whipping boy nor did I take pleasure in anyone thinking otherwise. Even as my colleague, if I thought that was your intention you'd have to send people on the council just to straighten me out. That's why I became city clerk. They wanted to get me off the council because they couldn't handle me.

The Problem with Favors

Based on what I've witnessed in my many years in politics, the subject of favors can be a tricky one. In fact, most politicians seeking to advance their cause by accepting a favor, usually end up having to betray the very cause they've sought to advance. The fact of the matter is that once someone has accepted a favor, (especially in politics) he is owned by whom he owes. Once money has been taken, it has got to continue being taken.

That is to say, while you can stop taking the money whenever you choose, there will be no difference in respect to the time from when you began taking it, be it 3 years ago or 3 minutes ago. Once you have taken the money, it can and will be held over your head. That is the way the politically corrupt operate. They move with the intention of using the party they "help" as a scapegoat, cleansing their hands in such a way that the person who takes the fall is quite often the person who also took the favor.

I did my best to stay out of that kind of mischief. I never put my hands on the money. I never so much as negotiated a contract, because I didn't want to get caught up in all scandal. That was my stance from day one when I walked into the council, because you could always get a good job if you wanted to roll over for one. But very few people could get a good job if they were just for the people.

On Talking

I believe it's wise to be cautious with who you even share your bits of pivotal information. Neither loyalty nor betrayal belongs to any one race. You do not have the asset of knowing who knows who. And if you're relying on your shade to save you, well, it's usually green that matters the most. Brothers and sisters sell out each other just like anyone else. And sometimes it's for trinkets.

In addition to avoiding covert saboteurs, a loose lip as it pertains to one's own business affairs greatly increases the risk of a leader becoming his own worst enemy. My personal philosophy is that, telling no one of your plans spares loved ones the guilt of betrayal and you the pang of regret.

Deliver Me from Those Liberals

In the world of politics, someone is always in search of an informant but if you're the sender beware the go-between is a "swinging door" of information and loyalty is usually not their strong suit.

This Is A Serious Profession. You In or Out?

It is not my policy to mentor any of the other council people. I may advise a few people here and there but ultimately, you've got to want to be on the council, "One thing about my political life is that even with all of the trials and tribulations I had, I was successful because of my determination to make it from the bottom to the top.

Whereas most people can't get the respect they deserve in a lifetime, I was able to get the most powerful position and run the show. I am of the persuasion that if you fail to convince someone you're capable, it's your fault!

If you cannot convince someone to give you that initial push then leverage is completely out of the question. And I previously stated, leverage is power and in this profession it's all about power. I had plenty of it at one time. It's a very difficult thing to go from the most powerful to limited power, in that you now are limited in your ability to get through to more people.

CHAPTER 18: HOW I SEE BEING A GOOD LEADER

Anyone attempting to obtain a position of authority for the right reason knows what they are essentially seeking, is an opportunity to be of service.

When managing a sizable staff, a leader must not be so focused on getting tasks done that he loses sight of the individuals performing them. I never allowed myself to become so sidetracked as to not periodically check in with my employees. I believe that it is the exclusive responsibility of the task manager to set a definitive example and pace for their employees. Should this occur to anyone seeking a leadership role in politics as too steep a demand, I would question their fortitude for the job.

And yet, I am not aloof to these challenges. I myself know personally the joy and pains of making a career in politics. Employees need and deserve to be heard. This is the way I see it...

Staying In Touch With The Needs Of The People

Sometimes it's easy to know what the people want. Sometimes they'll come to council meetings. And if the issue so happens to involve them directly, they'll show up raising hell, once in a while.

But if the issue doesn't directly affect them or they are unable to make a meeting I may receive a call telling me what the issue is and inquiries as to when and how I plan to do something about it. I rely on people reaching out to me to a great degree, because the people see what I don't. I can drive down your street 20 times a day and not see what you see. Therefore, I need someone to tell me that there's a pothole there or there's something else over here that needs some attending to. When I drive your down the street, I may not be in search of potholes or whatever the issue. I may have been searching for sanitation concerns or other issues. Yet, if I were looking for potholes then I would have seen them. But if not, I could drive down that same street nearly every day and miss them.

Humanistic Values

I have never understood how one could be a leader with claims of concern for the people, and yet not be ready to give of myself whenever called upon to do so. How could I call myself a servant of the public and not be willing to do everything in my power to better their lives?

I have found that while people respond to the talk they have even more respect for the walk.

Anybody can give you empty promises encouraging words, but it takes someone with a heart and mind for the people to get their hands dirty and fix it. My point of view is not only do I have to acknowledge a problem when it emerges, but once I have communicated that I am aware of an issue, my new dilemma is how to fix it.

Leadership

I have always had reverence for the Father above and have done my best as to adhere to his teachings. He was the only leader I felt I ever needed. It is my strong conviction that he has always been with me. He truly demonstrated this to me when at nineteen years old, I had a near death experience and walked away to tell of it.

When I say that I need no leader, it is for no other reason but that I have one. I believe everyone has one. So when you're looking for a politician or public servant, keep in mind that politics is a "people business" and the prerequisite is that they do something to better and move humanity forward and make evident their humanistic values.

You must have self-determination; you must accept and use the hand that is dealt to you. And while you may need support in your endeavors from time to time, you never need a leader.

Have Confidence

The job of a leader is to display confidence as well as focused. Self assurance is an asset when working in any capacity whether that of superior or subordinate.

However, the wise leader is ever cautious to never allow pride to cloud their judgment as it pertains to accepting help when the betterment of their public is at stake. Arrogance must never be confused with confidence. Though seemingly akin on the surface, the two couldn't have further origins.

In my estimation, arrogance is a caricatured show of confidence used to mask personal insecurity, while confidence has far less to do with ego and is genuinely rooted experience.

The self-assurance that I have exhibited in all my years of public service comes not only from my experience in politics, but from my faith in the father above, the great leader that has been guiding me all along. I believe that it is due to such internal leadership that I have set my heart and my talents on an occupation that affords me the opportunity to better the lives of not only my brothers and sisters of color, but of mankind as a whole. That is not to say my quest for equity and integration have in any way made me a push over.

I never questioned whether or not I could do the job; I questioned whether or not I could get it. I had to have at least one white vote in order to get the position of city clerk and that worried me. Fortunately that's when a woman, a lawyer came forward and told me she would vote for me. It was then that I decided that I would wait no longer to make my move.

Once someone commits themselves to you in that capacity, you must move. Otherwise you look foolish and incompetent. You must give them some kind of incentive to continue to hold their position as it relates to you getting the job. You can't just tell a person that shows an interest in you that you don't care or even drag your feet in the direction that they are trying to help you towards.

If taken by surprise, the most you can say to them is, "Could you at least give me a little time to consider it? I haven't really thought about it." And the reason I hadn't really thought about it, is not because I wasn't competent but because I didn't think that I could secure a white vote. However I did obtain one, and that was from a Democrat. At that time the council consisted of all Democrats.

Interpersonal skills are key when it comes to the corporate world, and that's where it differs from the political world. In the corporate world, the public does not get involved. The bigwigs tend to do what they want.

Yet, in the political world the public's business is government. You must prove everything to them in terms of what you're about and what your intentions are. In the corporate world, the leadership chooses the people but in the world of politics the people choose the officials. There's a huge difference between the two.

Regardless, leadership in both realms is not obtained through any other means than confidence in yourself and in your ability to take on the task at hand. The question that remains is, *how badly do you want it*? You've got to want it and you've got to work for it, and the only way to work toward that assurance it is to know the operation.

Open Door Policy

I had an open door policy simply because no one else had one. I have always a believer in being frank. As a leader I would ask myself, "What are they going to ask me or tell me that I can't handle?" And that left me with the only I responsible action I could take, listening.

If I heard that anyone had an issue with me, my approach would be to handle it as soon as I possible. In attempts to clear the air I would call them in to my office and ask them to explain the nature of the conflict and how we might resolve it together in order to reach a mutually benefiting solution. The bigwigs usually tend to hide behind doors. Most employees wouldn't see the inside of the boss' office unless they were in some sort of trouble. I had an open door policy because as an employee, I knew firsthand how it felt to carry certain unresolved issues and not be able to address the boss personally. I want to know how you feel as well as have you know how I feel so we're not in doubt about each other's thoughts.

My door, as well as my ears, was always open. That is not to say that my office was a chat room for small talk. I had no desire to hear any gossip or any such nonsense. If you came into my office to talk, the topic had better be work related. In the context of business, you could come to me virtually anytime and discuss whatever the problem was. I may not always tell you what you want to hear, but make no mistake about it, I didn't have a problem resolving any issues that were pertinent to making the work place more pleasurable and therefore more productive.

I find for the most part bosses tend to be passive aggressive. That is they'd rather ignore you than face your issue head on. I'd much rather face it. My main reason being that upsets within the office are important to me. I have a desire to know what the issue is immediately. I don't need to know two weeks from now, I need to know now.

For this cause, I try to make myself as available as possible. Because I am aware of the unpredictability even in the workplace. I know that there will be days when we both will be busy and a face to face meeting is not possible. The pace can speed up in an instant and no matter how hard you try or how committed you are, a meeting just won't be possible. This occupation isn't easy and it's not a game. Though I may refer to it as a game occasionally, I speak more in the realm of approach and state of mind.

Minding Your Business

Although the notion of seeking someone out personal information from an outside and personal source may seem a bit extreme, I had rivals would go to the extent of sending people to my friends and relatives. These liaisons would talk to anyone they felt could give them enough dirt to bury me.

Yet, the one thing that I would not allow is let me family get involved. I mean sure, you could go talk to my mother, grandmother, wife, children, whatever, and nobody would know enough to be able to tell you anything, because they didn't know anything. And that kept them out of this crossfire, this political danger zone. I've witnessed too many people be brought down because they were too loose with their work related business. They would make the mistake of having their wives and friends and everyone else involved in their operation.

The only problem with that is the next time you open up a newspaper, you've found that someone has said something to a reporter.

Albeit, the friend or family member may have released this information innocently, your personal business has still been disclosed and you may face an uphill battle attempting to rectify what may no longer be salvageable. That's where it gets a little tough. But I have managed to keep my personal affairs under a tight seal. I wouldn't tell anybody anything, and I kept everything close to the chest so that my loved ones had nothing to tell. That's always been my style.

Put Your Foot Down

Yes, there were major issues where I had a distinct split from my party. There were certain things they thought should be implemented that I didn't feel would be to the benefit of people of color.

However, once I established my stance as a politician they knew better than to try to dissuade me from my view. If I'd really made up my mind on a matter, they knew could forget about changing it. I was so resolute on a topic that could go to my house, my mother's house and quite frankly anyone who knew and they would tell them the same thing. They'd say to them point blank, "If he's made up his mind there's nothing I can tell him that's going to change it."

If a leader does not have resolve they are at once dismissed and viewed as a person of weak character who is indecisive and untrustworthy. No one believes in nor puts anything of worth in the care of a whimsical person. The most powerful individuals understand the power of fixity.

Own Your Decisions

I would imagine if I thought about it, I could find a few things that I could have been done better which may have made it easier for me or made it easier for people. I've often heard people say that hindsight is 20/20.

Yes, I've made mistakes and probably could have approached some things differently. I stand behind the decisions I have made. No matter how well you handle things I've found that there's always that someone there that will estimate that they themselves or other individual could have done better than you.

So I'm quite sure I made mistakes. I mean after all, I *am* human. At the very least, I know that every situation teaches you something. But because I know that I've always worked from integrity, I own my decisions.

Like Me or Not

The reason I got into so much trouble is simply because I never did anything out of my character. Even at the cost of popularity I did what felt true to me. I never did anything simply because it would make someone happy or so they would like me or give me a pat on the back. As it related to my colleagues especially, I couldn't care less whether they liked me or not. Because no man can serve two masters, this has been my approach to protecting the people I represent. On my political journey there was only one group of people I cared about gratifying and that was the community I was elected to serve.

CHAPTER 19: HOW I SEE RACE

The progressive society in which we live has at times, shown itself only so progressive. We are living in an age of technological advancement that has surpassed nearly all that we could have possibly dreamed of just thirty, twenty, or even ten short years ago. Today we have advancements that range from cars that can run on corn fuel, to cloning technology and beyond. And yet sadly, some things remain the same, like racism.

There is a struggle for pride that runs so very deep with blacks. And based on our history of humiliation and inequality in America, there is no wonder. Yet, when we do obtain that power, we're so quick to forfeit it for a name, for recognition of some kind that it renders us ineffective. Had I felt that I could do more for the people, in a political position of lower profile as opposed to a more visible one with less reach I would undoubtedly choose the former. As a public servant, you should be out there trying to improve everyone's quality of life—not just your own.

Without revenue or at the very least, a way to generate it the wedge between black and white was broadened even further. There was now a gap between rich and poor. In fact, during my travels to Europe I have been fortunate enough to learn about the socioeconomic class system and the close parallel it bears to racism. The irony is that the income-based division created between classes promotes not merely a gap between the wealthy and the working class but also the wealthy and the wealthy. From

Deliver Me from Those Liberals

the beginning of time, society has constantly been seeking out any excuse to divide itself. This is the way I see it...

The Delusion About Racism Today

Surprisingly, there are lots of people who allow their imagination, the mainstream media and TV sitcoms to lead them to believe otherwise, but I believe racism is worse now than it's been in any other period in time. I say this because the practice of racism especially as it pertains to the workplace is far more "hands free" than it's ever been. No longer does it appear in the noose segregated restrooms or the "N-word".

Instead it is reflected in the lower wages and the lower positions held the average black and minority working class. The reason being is that the old style of racism is far too sloppy, tactless and risky. Times have even change for those who take a more forthright approach regarding their biases.

Today calling certain white people racist is like giving them a badge of honor. In the past, calling them out wouldn't change what they did of how they felt either, but they were at least embarrassed by being called one. These days if they're a radio or TV personality they not only get to keep their jobs but are rewarded with more publicity and obtain higher ratings! Their response to such shameful accusations is, "You're just being sensitive." Or "Call me a racist, I am what I am!" How can you deny racism exists when the racists stand up?

Jack Drakeford

Experience Doesn't Always Equal Advantage

As city clerk I had the ability to review the resumes of all applicants, hired or not. Early on, I would review records and wonder why some of the more apt individuals didn't get the job.

I've since come to learn that usually applicants are denied jobs for two main reasons. Either they were overly qualified or they weren't qualified enough. In New York, (which I always use an example) we had at least four or five chances in the past four to five terms of mayors none of which had the credentials to be chancellor. Yet they were made so, because they got the necessary support. Not because they had the ability do the job but because they got the support to do the job.

This meant that they were taking orders from the very people that were relying on them to make things happen. And the sad part was watching them overlook my capable brown brothers and sisters and as if they did not exist. There had been some cases of injustice that I would ponder while patiently awaiting the right the moment to address them.

However, on subject of the fore mentioned instance, I could not even conceive of being given an answer to which I could apply reasoning. There was no explaining away that one. You couldn't tell me that a decision had to be made and so instead of giving the position to the most qualified prospect a decision was made from another perspective. How could such an important decision be made without any regard to the candidate's ability to perform the job in question?

Unfortunately, we at the time as minorities had no open floor to have such inquiries addressed. There was no there's no opportunity to say "I would like to challenge you on this or I have serious concerns about your having done that." We didn't get those kinds of chances, because we had not been sitting down at the right tables.

Blacks Sitting Down At The Right Tables

There are a few ways of getting to the right tables. Firstly, if you're a city official it already gives you latitude to get there. And being on the executive committee of any board is a sure fire way in. Sadly, that doesn't mean the racism is going to stop. There will be no end to the attempts to keep you out of the know.

Some board members will even go as far as to communicate by phone as to keep vital information unshared. And as long as the majority of the board members are not all talking on one line, then they're basically within the law to be exclusionary. So there are loopholes and many creative ways of getting around fairness. They are able to circumnavigate equity because doing so has been made fairly easy .

However, there are ways of staying in the loop but you cannot be passive. You've got to want to get around the barriers. You've got to want to find ways to get involved and make sure that you're being accounted for.

Jack Drakeford

You must make it your priority to be numbered. To ask the important questions, do your homework and attend the all meetings of which you are made aware. The reward of this type of tenacity is knowing that there's someone out there that appreciates what you're doing and wants you to know it.

Not only is keeping yourself in the know critical, but if you want to gain support of the public must know your ability and be confident about it. The public is not interested in hearing what you don't know and what you can't do. They are looking to hear what you do know and how it will better their quality of life. What they seek; what we all seek is someone who knows they can accomplish the task at hand, and is hungry to learn what they don't know and will stop at nothing in order to get the job done.

No one wants a leader who surrenders before they even get off the ground. If you, as a leader, are uncertain of your ability, then why wouldn't the public feel the same way about you? If you don't think you can do it, then why should I, as your boss, think any differently.

And yet, I have witnessed incidents in which they have knowingly extended a job to a minority knowing their credentials are lacking. I look at this type of mind game as nothing short of an attempt to fill a quota based on minority applicants. Then the powers that be can say, "We offered him the job, and he refused it." Now isn't that a liberating statement to be able to make? Or "We gave him the position and he fouled things up." Now, where's the

Deliver Me from Those Liberals

integrity or the civil service in handing the public an inept official bearing some likeness to their requests just to shut them up and prove them wrong?

However, if you closely observe politicians, you will be notice that the ones that try to get over on the public are usually the ones that get at best, get over on themselves. Once you sell yourself out, anybody who is privy to it will lose respect for you. If you're looking for respect, you must take a firm stance even at the risk of unpopularity. At least the public will know that you stand for something. It doesn't mean that you'll achieve everything they want you to, but at least you've revealed some commitment. And your display of that commitment will show the people your belief in them. If you don't believe in the people then you shouldn't even bother trying to represent them, that's how I feel.

The Struggle to Control Blacks

I do not find it farfetched, and believe it's quite evident that all throughout American history at there has been and still is a desire to control blacks. Just take a look at the different voting records of different black people. Take Randall Patterson for example. He's been a flatfooted black politician who would not give into popularity polls or submit to people's persuasions. In my opinion he should have made it to the top a long time ago. Yet, he never got there. Why? Because he took a stand but did not have the backing.

108

Jack Drakeford

Let's take a look at Charles Rangel. He was beloved by the people of New York. Whites, blacks, the community couldn't get enough of him. Yet he couldn't get as much as a nod of encouragement from the powers that be, to pursue these higher positions. Why? Because he did not fancy puppetry and wouldn't take any nonsense from them.

What must be understood, that there's a price you pay for speaking your mind. And the price you pay as an individual is the threat of being embarrassed, put down and slighted at every turn.

Now let's look at another well known leader of color, the minister of a well established historical church in Harlem, New York. When the mayor of the time said the only reason the minister didn't like him was because his administration prevented the building of a mall in Harlem. Not only would this 49 million dollar mall have brought revenue to the city, but it would have created jobs for countless minorities. The mayor, a long time foe, heard of the minister's involvement and cut off funding.

When I heard the news I felt terrible for him. Yet, I knew he had put himself in that position. He played the game of "you scratch my back I'll scratch yours" and he lost. Unfortunately he was no Adam Clayton Powell, in terms of understanding power. Butt's holds a lot of powerful positions and for economic purposes; he could most likely help lots of people. He's the head of one of the biggest churches that there is. Obviously, this isn't enough.

This man is carrying a big church with him, but he doesn't get half the leeway that Adam got, because Adam would tell you in a minute just how it is. He said, "If I don't see any of my people owning or at least working in or any of the stores on 125th street then my people will not be coming in there to shop. I've got some salespeople of color before you see my green."

When those types of conditions are placed on them the political bigwigs they don't want to hear them. But Adam if nothing else was a man that was in charge. That's often the problem with black politicians; they don't fully own the authority that comes with being in charge. Number one, you call a lot of shots and number two, you are responsible for a lot of money and jobs. When it's all said and done, as a politician, you're pretty in charge of much the all things that pertain to making society function, so act like it.

Sadly, many of the politicians of our time, white, black, and every color in between have had their focus far too fixed on green. That is not to say that money is not a valid interest. We all worry about finances from time to time. Yet, there is still the matter of your degree of concern around it. Too much worry and anxiety around money and you can find yourself in a world of trouble. And when that becomes the case, you have in essence said that money is of greater importance to you than your political future and your commitment to the public.

Jack Drakeford

Classicism and Racism

Many people may not be aware of it, but there is a divide between the rich. Those that have longstanding legacies and have established names are referred to as the "old money." While, those who have recently obtained wealth either independently through celebrity or through an inheritance are called the "new money." Those referred to as old money, are far more conservative in their spending than the new rich people of today. Years ago, you couldn't tell the people that were rich from those of the working class. They would wear the same clothes as everyone else and you would never know that they were rich, unless they told you themselves. They were affluent but never flashed money.

The rich of today are far more liberal with their spending. You can spot them from a mile away. From their big the cars and flashy jewelry to the designer clothing, they take great measures to make their financial status evident to all. In the military I learned all about the class system.

As previously mentioned, I spent 13 months in Germany. There the class system was taught very strongly. There, if you were born a peasant, you were going to die a peasant. There was no overcoming the poverty you inherited. It didn't matter if you were the best in the world at your trade. Which is exactly why most Germans were happy to see Hitler get into office. They figured they could possibly at the very least, get a fair shake. This was especially true for the peasants seeking to enter the mainstream.

It's not hard to see how the German's system of classicism runs parallel to the way that racism is dealt within our nation or any other nation. The only obvious difference between the two is that it's far more acceptable to address someone as a rich person than a racist.

Today, you have to be very careful as it pertains to accusing someone of being racist. It would be far less controversial to you say that you have a difference of opinion. I personally, will not deal with anyone racist. And if it were of absolute necessity to interact with them, I would at the very least limit my dealings with them. How am I supposed deal with someone, if I know they dislike me without a solid cause?

In my belief, the primary reason I got into hot water with certain white members of my party, is because they didn't stand for equity they stood for racism. I witnessed them using minorities to obtain and stay in power. I was never the one to buy into that. Why should I? Just because you're of a lighter skin tone, should that make you more qualified or more apt to serve a position than me?

When ran for city manager, I was called every name but a son of God. I was called "nigger", "darky", you name it. Yet, blacks were not the only ones that were being discriminated against. If they didn't like you because you were of Hispanic or Asian descent you were just as bad off as if you were black.

Jack Drakeford

To get to where I am, have allowed many slurs to roll off my back. But there was one word in particular that some might find the least offensive yet, was for me the last straw. And, that was the word 'boy.' I would never have allowed that to happen. I found that insult to be was totally unacceptable. If you call me 'boy' then most assuredly, without hesitation I'd answer you, but only the most offensive slur relative to your race of people that I could think of. I don't recall anyone having called me 'boy'. And I would never allow anyone think it was okay, even in jest.

This is mainly because I didn't play or joke with people. That is not to say that didn't observe social and exchange social pleasantries. I knew how to be sociable at the right times. But I didn't socialize very much. I maintained a clear level of professionalism at all times. My philosophy as it pertains to the work environment is that you've got to act like you're part of an operation. Do not mistake me.

I do not expect my employees to completely postpone being human for eight hours. However, I do feel that at least 90% of the time the focus should be on job performance.

CHAPTER 20: TODAY

I have witnessed and participated in many meetings in all levels of government. And I have yet to see where a political meeting would alleviate the real problems faced by real people. Instead, the focus is shifted to the business elements and political camaraderie. As for the betterment of the working class, the solutions they come up with are at best, like applying a band-aid to a deep gash.

Politics are an absolute must for the people of the world. Everyone should be involved on some level. I know that the prospect of approaching the world of politics can seem a bit daunting. But doesn't every new undertaking seem so at first? Like too many frightened and resigned people, you can also decide to keep your head buried in the sand. The way I see it is you can either choose to affect the world of politics or be forced to be affected by it.

Not many will be policy makers and public servants. Nor may many wish to be. But even the common constituent should not allow these rich political 'minorities' to speak for the masses of the poor and working class majority. And the politicians that have been bought speak for the corporations and special interest groups anyway, never the masses.

Of course, I am speaking from my personal perspective and out of the bounty of my own experience in the northeast's political structure. Yet, if we look at the metropolitan areas like New York, Philadelphia and

Connecticut, do we see any representation of the minority population?

The one thing I want the public to understand is that being an official or a political leader is a lonely and thankless occupation. Yet, the rewards can be enormous.

What most people fail to understand is that the political parties (Democratic or Republican) will not take care of you. Unfortunately, we expect our elected officials to make a difference without being monitored. This is probable but unlikely.

The truth of the matter is the chances that the government will make an impact in your life style without your involvement are slim to none. You must get in contact with your local politicians. You must show up at meetings and let your voice and opinion be heard. The actions of the government greatly affect your future. This is especially true for the average to below average income family.

Never accept any politician's individual mission statement nor should you accept the mission statements of political parties because they mean little to nothing in terms of solving problems. They simply play on the sentiments and emotions of minorities and average to below average income citizens. They know that these people are honest and usually expect the same. Often they tend to accept promises at face value.

I have always stated, you wouldn't allow your dentist, no matter how skilled, to perform open heart surgery. So why shouldn't you establish a criteria for public officials and appointed officials for lay people.

I must say that politics is a people business. So the prerequisite for being a public servant should be that one must have humanistic values. Because from my experience a humanitarian can learn politics but very rarely does one see a politician become a human being.

If within your own town, someone wanted to be, or thought there was a possibly that they had an interest in being on the council, there are ways of figuring it out for sure. Number one, they can test the water and see if the public and the council want them. Because without the public agreeing that you should be the person, it doesn't mean anything. That's the difference between the corporate and public service. In public service you do everything outside, you do it before the public eye, supposedly. That doesn't mean actually officials actually do, but they're supposed to.

So going to the public is and gauging their reception is the only legitimate way of knowing whether or not people will support you. You can affect an image or persona you like, but ultimately it is the people who assess your character and choose for themselves. This why I say that it's really surprising when I hear say people they don't know who they want to be as it relates to positions in politics.

Jack Drakeford

The fact of the matter is that they don't know their role as leaders for two reasons. Either they haven't given it thought, or they haven't tried to cultivate the team in operations in order to maximize their effort in terms of getting people to support them.

Most voters feel the best they can do to really hold elected officials accountable is not voting for them again. But it's so much more than just the ballot. If you really want to get involved in politics, you have to join organizations, join committees, something related to the party you feel strongly about, then you can have some voice inside.

If you're not sitting at the table then you have no input. Then you have no input, and you aren't represented. And when you aren't represented, you're forgotten. So stand up and be counted. Then shout loudly, and be heard. Help deliver me from these liberals...

AFTERWORD

I met Jack Drakeford in 1983 when I was running for the Council seat in the First Ward in Englewood. During my term on that council, we were looking for a new City Manager. The council appointed Jack Drakeford to be the interim City Manager while we did a search for someone to fill that position.

This was not the first time that he had been appointed interim City Manager, as well as performing his duties as City Clerk. During that process of the interviews, it seemed to me that Jack Drakeford could fill the duties of the job of City Manager as well as anyone. In addition, it did seem to be an advantage to have someone who knew the city and its citizens as well as he did and I wondered why we were wasting time looking elsewhere.

Never did I think that my decision to consider a vote for Jack Drakeford would cause such a stir. It was a shock to me how people who on the surface acted so open and fair-minded could harbor such racist tendencies. They came to my home and left threatening messages on my answering machine. They even involved my children in the nonsense.

In the end, I felt I had to do what was right. And stand up for my convictions. It was a good lesson for me, as well as my family. This was something I learned from Jack Drakeford—stand for something and do it with pride.

— Councilman Feinstein

59603176R00076

Made in the USA
Middletown, DE
12 August 2019